I'LL RUN WITH YOU

HOW GOD'S GRACE IS SUFFICIENT
WHEN *Our* STRENGTH IS NOT

WILLIAM BOYD CHISUM

MORGAN JAMES PUBLISHING • NEW YORK

I'LL RUN WITH YOU

ISBN: 978-1-61448-056-3 (Paperback)
       978-1-61448-057-0 (eBook)
Library of Congress Control Number: 2011929537

Published by:
MORGAN JAMES PUBLISHING
1225 Franklin Ave Ste 32
Garden City, NY 11530-1693
Toll Free 800-485-4943
www.MorganJamesPublishing.com

Cover/Interior Design by:
Rachel Lopez
rachel@r2cdesign.com

This book is dedicated to my "baby girl", the love of my life and keeper of my heart. Regardless the years that may come and go, in my life here on earth and forever in heaven, you will always be...

"MY RUNNING PARTNER"

ACKNOWLEDGMENTS

I want to take a moment to acknowledge a few people that have contributed so much to the writing of this book. First and foremost I want to recognize my Heavenly Father whose strength, grace and mercy have always been there for me, especially during those times that "The Advisary" said give in. His strength is always sufficient.

A big thank you goes out to my wife Nena and my son Brock, for allowing me the time to be locked away emotionally and physically while shackled to my laptop. Your patience and understanding over these long months help to make this book possible. I love you both.

Special thanks go out to my "older" brother James Andrew Chisum. Just as he carefully watched over me all those years ago, he is still, even today, taking care of "little brother." I never thanked you enough back then James, so hopefully this makes up for it in some small way. "You are appreciated and very much loved."

To my Mom and Dad who have walked "this long road" with me…I love you and I thank you both for always being that "Northern Star" that never failed to lead me back home each time I carelessly wandered from the path less travelled.

Karen Lewis, Founder and Creative Director at Simply Amusing Designs took an idea that had been floating around in my mind for over a year, and then brought it to life through the cover of this book. Thank you Karen for the hard work and "God given talent" you poured into this project. You created the perfect cover for this book. I believe the cover "Say's It All."

It is true that a writer cannot edit his own work. So, I was truly blessed when Martin Holland, from Great Britain, agreed to take on the daunting task of correcting all of my mistakes. I have never seen more "red ink" on any document in my entire life. But, because there is no better English, than THE QUEENS ENGLISH, his tireless efforts helped to make this book better than it would have been otherwise; and for that I will forever be thankful. Martin, you were the first to join my ever growing group of "running partners," and I look forward to seeing you someday soon.

To Wanda Anderson Pearson a.k.a (grasshopper), thank you for writing such beautiful words for the back cover. It is hard to sum up an entire book in under two hundred words, but you did it. Your friendship means the world to me and my family. Thank you Wanda for being a "Guru's grasshopper."

CONTENTS

FOREWORD

As a pastor of four Baptist churches for a total of forty-three (43) years, I have seen a lot of people whose lives are a testimony of God's power bringing triumph out of tragedy; people whose wounds become a witness to God's grace and power. Boyd Chisum is one of the people at the top of the list.

In "I'll Run With You," Boyd bears indisputable testimony to the truth that circumstances and events can be overcome; that difficulty doesn't mean defeat.

To anyone who's read Boyd's first book, *"Chasing The Wind,"* and thought that his faith in and faithfulness to God would grow weaker as his circumstances continued to be painful, here is his witness that his faith is strong and his hope is brighter than ever. In the scripture we are promised that God's grace is sufficient (2 Corinthians 12:9), that He will never allow His own to be tempted, tried and tested beyond our strength in Him (1 Corinthians 10:13). Scripture also reveals the one pursuit that every believer is to be engaged in: *"You will be my witnesses,"* (Acts 1:8). A witness is someone who speaks what they have personally observed or experienced. *"I'll Run With You,"* is a witness to God's Grace Saving us from sin, His Power

Sufficient to carry us through hardships, and His giving us a Soaring Hope of complete deliverance.

Your affliction may be different from Boyd's, Lacee's or Myrtle's, but God's promise is the same: *"These light afflictions… are not worthy to be compared to the glory that will be revealed in us."* (2 Corinthians 4: 17)

Read and experience the pain, see the hope and expect the fulfillment of God's promise—*"He will wipe away every tear from their eyes. Death will exist no longer; grief, crying, and pain will exist no longer because the previous things have passed away (Revelation 21:4)."*

Boyd, Lacee, Myrtle and All of God's Children, *"I'll Run With You, too!"*

Roy Ford
Pastor, First Baptist Church
Hooks, Texas

CHAPTER 1

Happy New Year
(GOD'S TIMING IS EVERYTHING)

I t had been only a couple of weeks since the Christmas concert at Scottish Rite Hospital for Children. That single event set the scene for a wonderfully blessed Christmas for the Chisum household. The opening of each present on Christmas morning brought back memories of the kids we had ministered to only days before. We couldn't help but feel thankful and fortunate for God's unmerited favor.

My father-in-law, Jack Moulton, had practically "camped out" at our house in the days leading up to Christmas. We were all excited as

I diligently put the finishing touches to my first book, *"Chasing the Wind"*. I was working on strategies on how to get accepted by a national publishing company. Being that this was my first book, the saying "He didn't have a clue" would be a gross understatement. It wasn't just that I didn't have a clue; I wasn't even sure where to start looking for one.

But God often answers prayers in ways that you least expect. And this was the case for me concerning the search for a publishing company.

I had received a phone call from Dr. Bob Bard a few days after Christmas. Bob was the Optometrist my wife Nena had worked for, for many years before our son Brock was born. He wanted to wish us a happy New Year and to ask if I would be interested in joining him on a trip to Atlanta, Georgia to an entrepreneurial conference. There would be many companies represented at this meeting, along with several nationally known speakers. As Bob began going down the list of guest speakers my ears "perked up" when he mentioned the name David Hancock, President/founder and CEO of Morgan James Publishing out of New York. I quickly wrote it down as Bob continued down the list.

To be honest, I really didn't hear much of the list of speakers after he mentioned Morgan James Publishing. I knew the possibility of me getting away and traveling to Atlanta was slim to none, so, after a few more minutes of conversation and with a quick check of my schedule I had to politely decline his invitation. As I hung up, I quickly began searching for information on this newly uncovered publishing company. Turns out, God was making sure I wasn't so clueless after all.

What I found on the Internet told me this was the right place for me to start. If I was going to get a ton of rejection notices (as everyone had been telling me to prepare for) then this was as good a place as any to start getting them.

Morgan James touted themselves as "A different kind of publishing company". Unbeknownst to me, these words would come into play heavily in the days that followed.

I couldn't wait to share this newfound information with my father-in-law Jack. He had committed himself to try and help me find a place for this book. He had spent so many long sleepless nights talking with me on the phone as I "two finger typed" my way through this autobiography. Jack and my wife, Nena, were both instrumental in keeping me going. They were there to encourage me when I felt I just couldn't finish it, or help me to write better when my fears of failure overwhelmed me, and all I could hear in my head was, "It was not good enough!"

I could best be described as a pit bull hanging on to a bone that New Year's holiday, because I would not let go of that publishing company I had shared with Jack; the same one he had procrastinated over calling for several days. All I wanted was information on their rules and processes on submitting a manuscript for review. It was on New Year's Day that Jack decided to call, and all along knowing there would be no one there to answer. He left a message requesting that someone call us back.

A day went by with no call from New York. Jack placed another call and then slowly the method behind the madness of a call on New Year's Day began to take shape. In the second message Jack left, he was very blunt and challenging. "I thought you were a different kind of publishing company but you're really not!" Jack said. "You claim to be a company that puts people first, but you won't even return a phone call," Jack went on. "I will believe you're different when I see it, and I'll see it when you return my call," and with that Jack hung up. It was less than twenty-four hours later when Jack's cell phone came to life.

The first call he received was from the secretary of Morgan James Publishing. She tried to explain to Jack that everyone had been off for Christmas and the New Year and that she was so sorry but even now there was no one available to speak with him. Jack erupted into what we affectionately knew as his "controlled temper-tantrum" and this only made the situation worse. Jack continued to repeat his earlier phrase to an overmatched and underwhelmed secretary, that Morgan James was not a "different" kind of publishing company. "You are just like all the rest," he said, and with that Jack abruptly hung up. My mouth must have been open so wide you could have flown a jetliner into it and not touched either corner of it. I couldn't believe my ears. "I wouldn't even get the benefit of a rejection letter now," I thought.

It wasn't twenty minutes later that Jack's cell phone began to ring again. I thought after the fourth ring that he wasn't going to answer it at all, but on the fifth ring he calmly said in the sweetest of voices, "Hello." This time it was David Hancock himself. Jack didn't act at all surprised; this was the man that he had wanted to, and had planned on talking to all along.

No one was too big or too important for Jack. He could talk to anyone. His fearlessness and polished demeanor, when on display, were amazing to watch. He often said, "Why should I be nervous to talk to anybody? I talk to God every day and there's no one bigger than He is!" The power of that statement is found in its simplicity.

Mr. Hancock was gracious and patient as Jack went through the story once again. "So what is it you want, Mr. Moulton?" was the final response from David. "Well, I want you to agree to publish this book," was Jack's 'to the point' response. One never had to wait long to find out where Jack stood on any issue, or learn what it might be that he wanted, because he'd let you know: and quickly.

David explained to Jack that Morgan James Publishing gets hundreds of submissions each year and selects only around fifty for publication. This did not dissuade Jack in the least and he let David know that basically, from this day forward, Morgan James need only to concern themselves with the other forty-nine books!

Before the conversation ended, David asked Jack to send *"Chasing the Wind"* directly to him. He didn't have time to review it himself, but he would direct someone on his staff to take a look at it and get back to us. He was very careful not to make any promises or commitments other than, "We'll see." When Jack hung-up the phone, I couldn't help but feel sick to my stomach. Rejection number one, I was sure, would quickly be on its way!

I watched the mailbox like a lunatic. I think our postman even began to feel like I was stalking him because I was watching him come and go with so much intensity. I would stand out in the yard waiting on him to drive up and actually got a little peeved each time he didn't hand me what I was waiting for. I think he was afraid that I was the one about to "go postal".

What would a rejection letter look like? Would the publisher be polite and say something like; "You almost did it, so keep working at it." Or would it be a letter comprised of only one sentence; "This stinks on ice"? I was sure it would be one of the two. Everyone knows that no author gets accepted on his first try.

In less than two weeks I received a letter with the MJ Publishing logo and address in the top left hand corner. It was your standard business size envelope and very light weight. I thought to myself as I carried it in to the house, "How heavy does a 'don't call us we'll call you' letter have to be?" I think I was holding the answer to that question in my hand.

I sat at the desk in my office and looked at the envelope for the longest time. I was afraid of what I would find printed on the page just inside. As I carefully tore it open I said a silent prayer; "Lord, let it be what You want it to be."

"William, Congratulations! Your manuscript proposal, *Chasing the Wind*, has been accepted! Welcome to Morgan James Publishing, LLC."

For the next twelve months life became a blur! We were juggling so many projects, trying to keep them all in the air, that is was by grace and grace alone that we were able to accomplish so much.

I started a children's book, *"The Story of God's Grace"*. It would come with a CD that would allow the child reading the book to sing along with the words on each page. Jack found us a children's book illustrator: Karen Skold, who lived in Sweden and spoke little English but her artwork was beautiful and absolutely perfect for this project. Her daughter, who was in college at the time and taking English classes, was able to translate for us. Karen delivered such moving artwork on each and every page, and when it was finished she refused to take any compensation for her hard work. She told me, "I did this for the glory of God," and I know that her reward will be great one day! Morgan James Publishing quickly accepted my second book and suddenly I had become a multi-published author.

Jack now turned his efforts to the gospel CD I had recorded earlier, also entitled *"Chasing the Wind"*. With the album now printed and several solo concerts on the books, it was time to find a record label that would be willing to sign a new artist. Oh, I really wasn't that new, I had been in country music, toured for many years and had chart singles across the country. But, now I was singing the songs God had laid on my heart and for the first time in my life, I was now listening to His direction. I guess I was a new artist after all!

Dave Moody was, and is, the president of Lamon Records with offices in Nashville, Tennessee as well as North Carolina. He also had the experience and notoriety of being a multi Dove and Grammy Award recipient for his producing abilities. Jack almost met his match in the "negotiating arena" when he and Dave went at each other over many phone conversations, but when the smoke had cleared I was signed to a Southern Gospel recording label and my first national release was only weeks away.

When God starts opening doors in your life, things often happen very quickly. It always becomes a situation that, when you look back at it all, you realize that only God could accomplish what was happening. I call it a "God Thing", and when He opens a door, no man can shut it. I was seeing an unbelievable amount of doors opening and even though I did not know where they all would lead me I had learned to trust THE ONE doing the leading.

The year was 2007, and I was looking at a list of the top fifty gospel songs in the nation, as reported by Singing News magazine. There, close to the bottom of that list, I found my name and my first release on Lamon Records; *"He Still Moves the Stone"*. Jack and I were sitting in the same restaurant where I had signed the publishing contract for my book. It was also the very same place we chose to sign my recording contract that took place barely two months later. Having the first release from my *"Chasing the Wind"* album make the charts was truly a humbling experience for me. Jack was so proud and for almost an hour went around showing everyone at each table the list of the top fifty, and making a "huge" effort to point me out.

Oh, I was excited, of course, but really more in shock than anything. You see, I had made God wait for so many years while I was busy singing songs that meant nothing, and added nothing to The Kingdom, that I realized that God was working overtime to show me what He could now do. How He could take my small contribution, if I would just let Him, and do exceedingly and abundantly more than I could ever have imagined.

Little is great when it is placed in the hands of God. Like the five loaves of bread and two fish, my gifts were being multiplied by God and used to feed a lost and hungry world with the very "Bread of Life".

Later that year, Nena and I received our voting ballets for both the *2007 Dove* and the *Grammy Awards*. Who would we vote for in the Southern Gospel Song of The Year Category? I wondered. Oh yes, I would be remiss if I didn't mention that *He Still Moves the Stone* was nominated for Song of the Year, so of course we voted for it. We weren't stupid, and it probably was the only two votes the song received. We didn't win, however, but oh what an honor it was just to be nominated.

God had been so good to us and we were thankful. We were truly being fed in the valley, where it was lush and green, but there was a mountain that would soon appear in our path. At the top of this mountain we would find emptiness. It would be a place of rocks and boulders where nothing could live. Climbing this mountain would leave us a family, bloody and scarred, and with wounds so deep they would never heal on this side of heaven.

CHAPTER 2

Jack's Lost Journey

There comes a time for each of us when we realize that we have given our all. Exhausted, we all too often continue to pour ourselves into a ministry, a Sunday School class or even an individual, and then we end up feeling more than just burned out; we are completely and utterly empty.

'Empty' best described my father-in-law Jack when it came to all the new aspects swirling around my ministry. Books, albums, concert schedules, speaking engagements: they all ran together and made Jack wonder if there might be something missing in his life. Had he given so much to my ministry to the exclusion of his own?

Maybe Jack could have paced himself a little better, but that just was not in his nature. He always went headlong into life at breakneck speed and you either ended up taking the ride with him, or you got run over. Oh, by the way, he was the worst driver I have ever ridden with in all my life; but then that's another story all together. But I will say this about it: when I would be white knuckling the dashboard as he weaved in and out of traffic at the speed of light, he would look at me and ask with a sarcastic smile; "What are you afraid of, aren't you prayed-up and ready to go home?" Well, I was, but I didn't think there was any need to hurry the process along.

Life with Jack was never boring, but maybe life with me had become so. Jack had reached the point where he needed to move on. He longed for another challenge, another deal. To him it was all about the art of negotiation that kept him fired up. He needed another spark.

The hardest part for Jack as he prepared to move back to Scottsdale, Arizona was twofold. Number one: how would he be able to say goodbye to his favorite grandson Brock? They shared a bond that was very special and, despite Jack's gruff demeanor at times, they loved each other deeply. Number two: where would he find someone to watch over him, love him and care for him more than his step-daughter Nena did? We knew that there was no safer place on earth for Jack than where he lived now, just two blocks from our house.

There was a great feeling of trepidation as we watched Jack make plans to leave. He had leased his condo, made arrangements to transport his Mercedes and packed the multitude of boxes that held all the pieces of his life. Each box would carry a piece of Jack across the country and far away from us. We felt helpless but nothing we could say or do would change the course Jack was determined to follow.

There seemed to be a void in Jack's life, and he didn't know what was causing it. He just believed he needed to return to that place where he thought he was happiest and maybe there he would find who it was or what it was that could fill the emptiness he was now experiencing.

We watched him drive off early one morning. Our hugs goodbye seemed a little forced and stiff. It could have been because he knew we didn't want him to go, and felt the journey he was now on might not end well. That deep blue Buick Grand Prix that I had so many near death experiences in, was now driving away. For as I long as I live I wouldn't miss the rollercoaster ride that I found within those four doors, but oh, how I would miss the man behind the wheel.

Months went by and we heard very little from Jack. The little dribs and drabs of information that we received from him over those months always seemed to have a glaring hole. He said that he was very busy meeting old friends and seminary buddies and together they were actively working on ministerial projects and outreach ministries. He had even had some of his writings become part of an on-line bible course for some University somewhere. But nothing could calm that uneasy feeling within our hearts that something wasn't right.

January 30th started out like any other day, answering e-mails and returning phone calls. As I sat in my office, sipping on my third cup of coffee, the phone rang and I recognized the number immediately. It was Rev. Bud Brown: the one who helped me dig a little deeper in the writing of *Chasing the Wind*. He was the associate pastor of the fastest growing church in the United States, located in Sedona, Arizona. He was also one of Jack's closest friends.

In a somewhat surprised voice I said, "Hello Bud", because I had not spoken with Bud since just before Jack moved away and with Arizona's time difference it was unlike him to call at such an early hour. "How are things in the land of enchantment?" I asked, but I only heard a long silent pause as his response. When he finally spoke, his words were careful, controlled and almost seemed rehearsed: "Boyd", he said, "Jack committed suicide this morning around 3:00 AM".

The phone began to tremble in my hand, as I fought to keep my emotions in control. I was trying my best to understand the information Bud was conveying on where Jack's body was, what the police were doing and how the investigation was going, but all I could hear, reverberating like white noise in the background, was that "Jack was dead!"

After Bud hung-up the phone I took a brief moment to collect my thoughts. I had to call Nena at work and tell her to come home. I couldn't break this news to her on the phone; she had to be here face to face where I could try to help hold her together as she fell apart.

Nena answered the phone and I simply said, "You have to come now." I didn't want to tell her while she was at work, but she insisted. With a cry that came from somewhere deep within her, she said, "I'm on my way home."

I was concerned about her emotional state; coupled with the forty-five minute drive it would take her to get home. I knew her mind would be racing to try and figure out this tragedy that had smashed its way into our lives. Why had he done this? What was so bad that he couldn't call us for help? All of these questions and many more kept her company on her fast yet unremembered drive home. Now she was sitting in my office, with mascara-streaked cheeks and a heart shattered into more pieces than I could possibly put back together.

Nena and I debated on just how much to share with Brock. We finally decided that he was old enough to know the whole truth. We couldn't lie about the details surrounding Jack's death because inevitably someone would slip up in front of Brock, and ask the question, "Why did he do it?" We prayed that God would give us the words we would need to share with Brock about the ugliest side of life and death that he would ever know.

When Brock came in from school we sat him down on the same couch in my office where Nena had received the news just hours before. I told Brock that his Papa Jack had died and his first question of course was, "How?" As I shared the information about Jack's suicide, Brock cried and clenched his fists and began waving them in the air at an enemy he could not see, as he cried over and over, "Why? Why? How could Papa Jack do that to himself; how could he do that to us?" It was a plea for an answer from a confused little boy that in the span of mere seconds had to grow up in ways that a little boy should never have to grow up.

We didn't know that Jack had been in the grips of deep depression for several months. He didn't allow us in to that place where we could have seen how lost he was in his journey. Life was not what he had thought it would be back in Scottsdale and Jack realized he had made the worst decision of his life in returning there. Why he felt he couldn't just pack-up and come back home to us I will never know.

In the early hour of the morning on January 30, Jack R. Moulton took his well-worn Bible and opened it to one of his favorite verses. In a room all alone, with the open Word in his lap, Jack took a pistol and ended his life.

Oh, how I wish Jack could have heard what I heard in my mind on the banks of Lake Ray Hubbard several years earlier. With my gun in hand, I was prepared to end the pain I was going through too, but it was the words of the song *"Because He Lives I Can Face Tomorrow"*, softly floating on the wind and across the water, that ultimately caused me to realize that Jesus paid a high price for my life and I could not end that which no longer belonged to me.

It does not matter how strong you think you are in the Lord. If you know Christ, and are trying to serve Him, then the devil is coming after you and you are no match for him on your own. Jack, with his Doctorate Degree in Theology, was still vulnerable in the throes of his depression, to the one who walks this earth seeking whom he may devour.

I don't have all the answers to share with you as to why Jack did this. I do know that when I see him in heaven one day, I will first kick his butt before I hug his neck! But, if there is anything that my family and I can share with you the reader, on this chapter, it would be this: if life gets hard and you feel lost and alone, please remember what Jack seemed to have forgotten—you can always come home!

CHAPTER 3

Closer Than a Brother

PROVERBS 18:24

I n November of 2007 I had been asked to produce a Christmas "liner", or a Merry Christmas commercial if you will, for SonRise Radio in the United Kingdom. Paul Woodland, the radio station's founder and main DJ and I had come to know each other well since *"Chasing the Wind"* was released for air play "across the pond". At one point in the most requested songs that year, the songs of *"Chasing the Wind"* held seven of the top ten spots. Never had it been done before, nor has it been done since. After that wonderful blessing the song that Brock sang on, *"That's What Fathers Do"*, became the most requested song on Sonrise Radio for eleven straight weeks. So, of course I would do this Christmas greeting.

Paul also wanted me to round up a couple of other groups from the USA to add to this sixty-second spot. Seeing how I was dealing with musicians (there were no drummers involved) it would take some creative scheduling but in the end we all showed up at the studio at the same time and, surprisingly enough, on the same day!

The two groups that Paul had requested be a part of this commercial were The Mid-South Boys and Southern Grace. Each group had songs that were being played steadily in the UK and both had developed substantial fan bases of their own. We all met in early December at Smart Production Studios, and this would be the first time I had met either group face to face.

Everyone was professional and business like and the commercial was finished in just a couple of hours. But to be honest, with most of the guys in Southern Grace not knowing me; the Mid-South Boys not knowing Southern Grace, and, with the exception of Roy Dale Bray and Chip Bricker, I didn't know any of them; I think we were more comfortable with our friends in the UK than we were with each other!

Now, "There is a friend who sticks closer than a brother" and even in those times when he is not by my side, I can still talk to him on the phone. It had been seven months since we recorded that verbal Christmas card to the UK. Roy Dale was calling to see if I wanted to be a part of a multi-card Gospel show in New Boston, Texas during their annual Pioneer Days Celebration on August 8, 2008.

Now understand something here: Roy Dale is my brother just as surely as if my mother had given birth to him. We're always there for each other in times of grieving and great rejoicing. Funerals, weddings, and of course the baptism of my son Brock; Uncle Roy Dale was there. Having Roy Dale, his wife Barbie and their beautiful girls Ashley and DeAnna present at Brock's special occasion only increased the beauty of, and enlarged our family tree.

Roy Dale went down the list of the soloists and groups who would also be at the concert that night. I was excited to hear that the group Southern Grace was one of them. Roy Dale was singing baritone for this quartet along with "The pianist and producer extraordinaire", Chip Bricker.

With the exception of that December sixty- second commercial, I had not heard Southern Grace perform and I was looking forward to hearing my friends Chip and Roy Dale once again. I had a long musical history with both of these men going all the way back to *"The King's Four"*; a gospel group we were all blessed to be a part of, long before Brock was born.

The night of the Pioneer Day concert I had set up my product table just outside the auditorium. Due to a lack of space for each artist, Southern Grace and I ended up sharing a table. That was fine with me because it would allow me a chance to get to know the other three men in the group: Mark Hancock, Joe Ayers and Don Peace.

Southern Grace's music was "straight up; downright, slap yo mama, fried chicken on the grounds, southern gospel"; the style of music where the tenor raises the roof of the church and the bass shakes its foundation, leaving the lead and baritone searching for a place to hide. Who says you can't have fun being a Christian? And, with Roy Dale providing the comedy relief for the group, followed by the unpredictable antics of the event's emcee Mike Powell, it was obvious that the crowd got their money's worth. Oh, wait a minute; it was a free concert!

As I sat at the product table I began getting to know the rest of the guys in Southern Grace. Mark was the lead singer and front man, and it didn't take long into our conversation for me to realize that Mark had a heart for the lost as well as those who were "dead in Christ". The term "Dead in Christ" is one I often use to refer to those who are "warming a pew, but they're not on fire".

Don Peace played the bass for Southern Grace and was the road manager, booking agent and one of only two of its founding members still living. Well, that's not actually true, but it is a standing joke within the group concerning Don and the only other member I did not yet know, Joe Ayers. "Don't you just love old people?"

Don was ex-military and he had that "get it done" personality. His broad smile and quick handshake or a firm pat on the back made everyone feel at ease when they were around him. He had sung baritone for many years for Southern Grace, until his organizational talents became essential to the growth of SG's Ministry, and so he obediently took on the reins of manager. But he would continue to play his bass guitar on stage with the group until (just like Charlton Heston once said) they pried it from his cold, dead hand.

The first thing I noticed about Joe Ayers was he was everything I was not: tall, thin and always impeccably dressed. I mean the kind of man who could always tie his tie so that it came down perfect to the buckle on his belt, and never a millimeter off either way. My ties, when I wore one, were always hit and miss. Some days I looked like Laurel and Hardy, and then on others, more like "String Bean".

But out of the entire group, Joe was the hardest to read and the least forthcoming on whom and what he was about. Joe hardly spoke unless he was spoken to that night. I don't believe that was because he didn't want to be friendly, because he was friendly. But his quiet demeanor seemed to me to be just a part of his personality. He appeared to me to be the kind of guy you could go to if you weren't paying attention to something and ask 'what did they say?" and I'd bet a hundred percent of the time, he'd repeat it back to you verbatim.

Overall, it was a great night getting to know the members of Southern Grace. Just being around Chip and Roy Dale again was not only refreshing to the soul but it brought back great memories of the countless songs we had sung and places we had been. It also led me to re-examine all the huge pieces of our lives, and the reservoir of time that we shared with each other.

Another Christmas and New Year had come and gone, and all the roadwork and solo concerts were taking their toll on my legs. My soundman, roadie, bodyguard, traveling companion and all around "nice guy" Steve Oglesby, was doing his best to make it as easy for me as he could. But, a lifetime of surgeries will only make your body turn on you and fight back as you get older. And wouldn't you know it; I had just celebrated another "happy birthday", though they seemed to be getting a little less happy each year!

January 31, 2009 found me at home, contemplating where my ministry was going and how in the world could I continue, given my increased pain and decreased mobility? I always said, "If I ever get to where I can't walk or even sit down, then just clear off a place and let me lie down and I'll tell you how God has always made a way, where there was no way." Well I hadn't reached the lying down part quite yet, but still my God was busy "making a way".

On the other end of the phone line was Chip Bricker, calling from somewhere out on the road. "Do you want to be the lead singer of Southern Grace?" he asked. Before I could answer he started in again, "Mark just gave his notice just three minutes ago because he is taking a new job out of town, so Roy Dale and I jumped off the bus to give you a call. Do you want to?" He was talking so fast it was hard to keep up. I said, "I don't know, I guess I could for a while till you find somebody." Chip quickly replied, "What do you mean? We just did!" I don't remember the conversation ending because, just as quickly as he began talking, he shut-up and hung up!

With that, I became the lead singer of Southern Grace. Oh it wasn't that easy of course. It never is when you're dealing with scheduling issues and new personnel. I also had my solo concerts that had to be figured in and they had theirs. The fact that I lived in Dallas and they were based out of Texarkana didn't help either. Getting together for rehearsals would require me to drive three hundred and thirty two miles round trip. I spent more time driving than practicing. I can hear the reader's mind now saying, "Well that explains a lot!" But listen, when it's God that opens a door, then no man, no amount of problems and no degree of uncertainty can join together enough to close it.

I had what seemed to me to be an endless number of songs to learn. It wasn't just learning all the songs that I sang lead on but I also had to learn all the harmony parts to the songs that Joe, Roy Dale and Chip sang the lead on. Mark's last concert with Southern Grace would be on February 8, 2009 and my first concert as their lead singer would come all too soon on March 8, 2009. There was a bright silver lining however to that dark opposing cloud over my head; Mark Hancock was willing to help "walk me through" the maze of songs, skits and diverse personalities that collectively made up Southern Grace.

If it had not been for Mark's friendship and unselfishness, I could have never pulled it off. There was a strong connection between Mark and myself. I think it was that we shared a "kinship of spirit" to reach the lost and hurting. That connection grew stronger in the four weeks that we worked tirelessly to make this transition of "voice and men" as seamless as it could be.

Early on the morning of March 8, and much too early for my neighbors, I'm sure, the Southern Grace tour bus weaved its way through my neighborhood to pick me up. We were headed for "back to back" concerts in Desoto, Texas and then Rendon, Texas. A new page had been turned in my life. I climbed on board what was affectionately called the "Blue Goose" as the newest member of Southern Grace. Together we flew down interstate thirty-five, charging into whatever blessings God had in store for us all.

CHAPTER 4

A Bridge for a Beautiful Heart

Funnel Chest sounds a little like the name of a carnival ride on the midway of your local county fair. Or maybe some tasty calorie laden, powdered sugar coated dessert, that's guaranteed to keep you "hyped up" on a crystalline-carbohydrate. Oh, how we wished it was that simple. Maybe this layman's term was meant to take the fear out of the condition's actual name: Pectus Excavatum.

Our son Brock started showing signs of Pectus Excavatum by the time he turned five years old. This condition is more common than one would expect and is basically when the sternum becomes concaved and dips deep into the chest cavity. Most people who have this condition never have any adverse symptoms other than the obvious cosmetic malformation. There are a small percentage of sufferers, however, who will experience severe complications, such as: a compressed heart, causing prolapsing of the valves thus reducing cardiac output, overall decreased lung function and poor oxygen distribution. When it becomes this bad, short of a miracle from God, the only way to extend a child's life is a surgery that resembles something straight out of medieval times.

We were told when Brock was five years old that his heart was fine, and that because his excavatum was slight at that time, his heart would just move a little out of position to accommodate the intruding sternum. He wasn't exhibiting any pulmonary issues or cardiac problems at all, so we were advised to keep a close eye on Brock as he grew, especially around the age of puberty, because things could change rapidly. When his lips began to turn blue with exertion and he started complaining of chest pains and experiencing heart dysrhythmias at the age of thirteen, we knew instantly we had reached the point where hard decisions had to be made. We now found ourselves facing a life and death scenario concerning the light of our life; and all of this came crashing in on us just four months after I joined Southern Grace.

Brock was growing so fast. He was already five foot and eleven inches tall when he turned thirteen. Nena and I were now looking up to our child, quite literally, and through this impending storm he was looking down at us, hoping we had the answers that would make things alright.

Having to make such a choice for your child, and knowing the effects of that choice would cause them more pain than they had ever known before, leaves you weak in the knees and with a constant feeling that you want to throw-up. I was now experiencing symptoms from the same disease that my parents had contracted many years earlier, the disease of "helpless fear".

We were able to rearrange a couple of Southern Grace's concerts so that I could be where I was most needed, with Nena and Brock. Together, Nena and I did an endless amount of research on the procedure that the surgeons at Children's Hospital of Dallas were getting ready to perform. The surgery was developed by Dr. Nuss and bears his name, the Nuss Procedure.

I previously mentioned that the surgery seemed to be something straight out of medieval times, and that's true, but it was far better than the earlier technique. Prior to the Nuss Procedure, the breastbone had to be removed completely from the body. Then surgically, pieces of bone would be taken out and reshaped, and then slowly, segment-by-segment and rib-by-rib, they were implanted back into the chest. This procedure left tremendous scarring on the patient and also suffered a very high failure rate.

The Nuss Procedure didn't require the complete opening of the chest, so that was the good side of it, but there would be more internal risks associated with it.

The plan for our son was that they would make two small incisions on either side of his chest, nipple high, and six inches down from each armpit. Then they would push an arthroscopic cutting tool with a camera attached, completely through his chest from one side to the other. Making a tunnel just a millimeter above his heart and lungs called for steady hands. One slip, one mistake and they would "nick" the sweetest heart I had ever known or could feasibly collapse the lungs of our boy, who had just now began to sing for Christ.

At this point in the procedure they would fill the thoracic cavity with a gas that would expand the chest wall in order to create a space between the heart, lungs, sternum and ribcage. The side effect of this would be experienced after surgery, due to creating a man-made version of pleurisy; but this form of pleurisy would be a thousand times worse.

A titanium bar would be molded and shaped, looking like an arching bridge, to match the shape that Brock's chest should be. When it had reached the desired shape through bending and twisting, it would be inverted like a U, inserted into the body, and then pushed through his entire chest. Once that had been accomplished, handles would be attached at each end of the bar, and while still in a U shape, with the arch towards the spine, it would then be inverted with great force. The U shape would be "flipped" into an arch or a bridge, if you will, just above the heart. The force of that inversion would end up breaking Brock's sternum along with all of his ribs that were attached to it. But it would return the chest into the normal shape God had intended for it to be. Sometimes I think ignorance is bliss and through all our research we suddenly realized that we had reached a point where we "knew just enough to know too much!"

Nena's mom, Kaylla, had arrived at our home the day before Brock's surgery. One more time she was standing in the gap with her great strength and love. She had been there for those major "marathon" surgeries that I had gone through in Phoenix as well as the "rebuild" surgery by Dr. Lancaster and Dr. Medlock in Dallas. She would continue even now, through Brock's surgery, to provide the support we needed and stand always at the ready with that reserve of strength, for when ours had run out.

Thursday morning on June eleventh 2009, we headed for the Children's Hospital in downtown Dallas. Dr. Hicks, Brock's surgeon, had scheduled the surgery for 10:00 AM that morning. The preliminary blood tests and chest x-ray that had to be done before surgery were time consuming, but it kept our minds busy with mindless details. All of this was routine and familiar to me and somewhat so for Nena as well; but it was completely different watching our only child goes through it.

Out of all the instructions and information that Brock had been given about this surgery, there was only one thing that seemed to bother him. He was not overly afraid of the pain that most assuredly would come, nor was he really concerned about the six inch needle that would inserted into his spine and remain there for several days after surgery. No, the one thing that seemed to saturate and permeate his every waking thought was the catheter they would place into his bladder. I explained to Brock that the catheter would be put in while he was asleep, and he would never feel it. Being the bright boy that he is, the following question came bouncing back almost before I had finished my statement; "And just how are they going to take it out?" Needing a break from the seriousness of that day, I simply told him they would grab the catheter, wrap it around their wrist a time or two, and then run from his room out into the hall until it all came out. Laughter erupted from everyone. Except Brock! He saw no humor in it and was obviously not happy, not happy at all!

Before they came to take him to surgery, they gave Brock a liquid tranquilizer. It was the children's version of an adult's "don't give a damn shot". Not only did this keep Brock calm as he waited, but it would also act as an "eraser" to his memory of all the details yet to come. He would remember very little of the events leading up to surgery. Nena and I both wondered where the line started so that we might be able to have a sip or two of that "amnesia elixir" ourselves, because there would be things we would like to forget as well.

Together we followed Brock's bed down the hall towards surgery. They stopped just short of the OR entrance, and in front of the electric double doors, in order that we might kiss Brock goodbye. How do you let go of your child in times like this? You really don't; you just physically place him in the hands of someone else and then you hold on with your heart.

Shortly after Brock had disappeared through the doors to surgery, Dr. Hicks came to talk to us. Nena took hold of the hand that now held Brock's life in it, and she said, "Dr. Hicks, I prayed for you last night and again this morning, and I know Brock is in great hands." Dr. Hicks just smiled and he shared with us something that would help to bring the comfort we needed. He said, "No matter what happens in surgery this morning, I will be treating Brock as if he were my own child." I guess we couldn't ask for more than that from Brock's surgeon. But what we were pleading with our Heavenly Father for, was everything; "Lord, please don't take our child from us."

~

Sometimes late at night I watch him sleep
I dream of the boy he'd like to be
I try to be strong and see him through
But God who he needs right now is You
Let him grow old
Live life without this fear
What would I be
Living without him here
He's so tired and he's scared
Let him know that You're there

Can You hear me?
Am I getting through tonight?
Can You see him?
Can You make him feel all right?

If You can hear me
Let me take his place somehow
See, he's not just anyone
He's my son

Lyrics by ~ MARK SCHULTZ

We sat, prayed and waited. I talked with God, asking Him to comfort my child and calm his fears. I knew all too well the thoughts of a child placed in this situation. I knew that no matter how much the surgical nurses stroked his hair and talked sweetly to him or held his hand; it would not calm the fear of being in such a strange place as an operating room. Everything there is frightening and he would be lost without the strength from his mom and daddy. I wanted so badly to take his place, endure this for him, but this time all of my determination wouldn't be enough. But, although Brock might physically have to walk through this storm by himself, spiritually he wouldn't be alone. From the day that he accepted Christ, he would never again be alone.

As I sat in silence I thought of all the things that I had endured as a child. I thought of the number of hours in my lifetime that my parents must have waited, like we were waiting now, for news of my condition. I also began to realize that maybe, just maybe, all of my surgeries were meant for just this day. Could that be true? Could it be that my whole life had lead me to this point so that I could use the experiences of my life to help my son make it through this experience in his? I closed my eyes and thanked God for all I had endured in my life and, if this was indeed the weaving of my life into Brocks, then it was all worth it.

The two hours of Brock's surgery seemed to last a lifetime. In my mind I kept going over the steps of this surgery: step one- making the tunnel through his chest, step two-filling his thoracic cavity with gas, step three- molding the bar just perfect for the correction needed, steps four and five- inserting the bar through his body and then the bone breaking rotation of that bar, and step six- suturing the bar into the ribcage on both sides. As I went through the surgery in my mind, I tried to remove the picture of Brock's face in each step. I tried over and over again, but I could not erase the face of our son lying impaled by a titanium bar.

Watching the clock, we held our breath and waited to receive word that the surgery was over. Just when we couldn't keep it in any more, the phone rang in the surgery waiting room. The volunteer manning the phone called out our name and said, "Dr. Hicks will be out to speak with you shortly." Exhale and inhale, we were breathing again!

Dr. Hicks told us that the surgery had gone well and they had successfully corrected Brock's pectus excavatum. "This is one of the worst cases of cardiac compression that I have ever seen." Dr. Hicks said. He then showed us pictures that were taken as they made the tunnel through Brock's chest, showing proof of his statement. Only a third of Brock's heart was even visible due to the depth of his breastbone. Brock's mitral valve was prolapsing; in other words, the blood was backing up into the valve instead of going out through the pulmonary artery. His lungs were also being compressed and could not inflate to their full capacity. Then Dr. Hicks produced the "after" picture. This picture showed the bar, now fixed in place, lifting up the sternum like an "arched bridge", and exposing a hundred percent of Brock's heart. I pointed out to Nena and Kaylla that if you looked real close at this picture of Brock's heart you could clearly see Jesus living there!

Before Dr. Hicks left us he said, "Your son has just undergone the most painful procedure we can do to the human body, and the next few days are going to be hard for him and you. We have assigned a team of four doctors who specialize in pain management," he went on to say, "and it will be their responsibility to keep Brock comfortable." It would end up taking a cocktail of three drugs through his epidural along with intravenous and oral pain meds to keep the pain of what he endured that day at bay.

Waiting in the hallway, we could see Brock in his bed being pushed towards us. We couldn't wait to get our hands on him, and see for ourselves that he was fine. Nena bent down over his bedrail and kissed his cheek. She reached out and quickly pulled the cover away in order that we might see how his chest looked now; and what we saw shocked us to the core. We were gazing down upon the most perfect looking chest we had ever seen. The physical benefits of this surgery would take months to play out but the cosmetic change was instantaneous. No longer would Brock be ashamed or embarrassed to go swimming with his friends. He would never again feel the need to keep his shirt on in order to hide what he knew would bring stares, laughter and ridicule. He was absolutely perfect!

Back in Brock's hospital room, Nena took up permanent residence. She was determined to not leave Brock's side until he was ready to come home. The room was not equipped for the three of us to stay, so it was decided that I would go home and sleep each night and return for my shift each morning. That meant that Nena and Kaylla were supposed to go home and rest each day but they rarely did. At most they would go home and take a short nap, get a shower, and then they'd be back. By the third day we all felt as if we had aged ten years and in fact, some of us were beginning to look like we had.

It took the first two days to finally get the pain medication just right and it was a good thing they did because Physical Therapy was coming around to get Brock out of bed to walk. Just standing up with that bar running through his body had to be extremely uncomfortable.

Then the real "dungeon torturers" showed up: respiratory therapy. This department of "pain producing blowhards" came around at least two times in the daylight hours and twice again each night to help Brock breathe. You try deep breathing with all your ribs and sternum broken! Brock hated it when they came around but he always tried his best and suffered his way through each inhale and exhale. It had to be done in order to keep pneumonia from setting in to his traumatized lungs.

Yes, he "toughed" his way through each step, and I was amazed at his endurance and courage. I was also impressed with Brock's character as he dealt with all this. Even when he was hurting so bad, he never failed to thank those who came to help him. He was so gracious in the midst of his ordeal, and he never forgot, not one time, to show his gratitude to those who rarely get the appreciation they deserve. The staff at Children's Hospital was observing a clear picture of Brock's heart; and they didn't have to see the surgery photograph to get it.

I was also humbled as I watched my wife. The pain in her eyes as she cared for our son was more than obvious; it was downright hard to miss. There is an inner connection between the souls of a son and his mother. Its existence surfaces from time to time and is completely visible in times just like these; when a mother has to stand helplessly by and watch her son as he suffers. I thought about Mary, the mother of Jesus, and how she must have had that same look of desperation, fear and exhaustion on her face. The anguish she felt as she knelt beneath the cross where her baby boy was now being crucified surely must have been what triggered the look on Nena's face each and every time Brock cried out in pain.

The mental picture of Mary at the foot of the cross is, to me, some of the greatest proof that Jesus was and is who He said He was. Why? Because a mother will say and do almost anything to stop their child from hurting, and if Mary was not looking up at the son of God, but rather just a man instead, hanging on that cross, then there is nothing that could have kept her from crying out "Please stop, it's all a lie!" Mary would have broken her silence if Jesus had not been the Messiah, The King of kings and Lord of lords. But praise God HE IS, and she didn't. That's just one more sign that proves it to me, because on the day of Brock's surgery I know that Nena would have walked through hell itself if it would have taken Brock's pain away.

Third day post-op and Brock was beginning to surprise them all. The pain management physicians were amazed at how well Brock was doing. They shared with us that never in all the years that they had been performing the Nuss Procedure, had there been a child recover so quickly and do so much so soon. We knew it was a testament to the outstanding care that the nurses and staff had been providing to Brock, coupled with the countless answered prayers from all over the world. Prayers from England, Sweden, and from Okinawa to Australia; they were all a vital part to his astounding recovery.

The more ambulatory Brock became, the less he would need his catheter. I could not help but laugh when his eyes became as big as saucers the day the nurse came in to his room to remove it. I caught a glimpse of that "I'll get you look" as I calmly stepped out into the hall. When the "tug of war" was over and the nurse had ultimately won, I re-entered his room where his I'll get you look had now changed to a look of appreciation; thankful that my vivid description of how it would go had not come true.

The third and fourth days after surgery were filled with family and friends coming to visit. My mom and dad came; in spite of dad's dislike of how "city people drive" and Dallas traffic in general. They both had to see for themselves the change in Brock's chest and how he was doing. One of Brock's closest friends, Colin Grigsby, came along with his whole family. In fact, they came to check on him over several days during Brock's stay at Children's. There is something about a best friend caring about you, which makes life in general a better place, even if that place is stuck in a hospital.

On the evening of the fourth day of Brock's hospital stay, his pain doctors came in and informed us that they were going to remove his epidural line. Brock was now doing so well; they felt as if they could keep a handle on his pain through oral medication alone. For a thirteen year old who had been on a cocktail of three epidural medications as well as Oxycotton and Valium, we felt as if we had reached a huge milestone in his recovery.

Brock followed their instructions and leaned forward as best he could. The fact that they wanted him to arch his back and scrunch up into a ball, made Brock protest a little, but in spite of the pain, he did it anyway. With one long pull the epidural was out of his spine and he was now able to lean back into a sitting position, which was a little more comfortable than before.

That night the only pain medication he requested was what he had grown to affectionately call "The V Pill". Valium was his friend on the days when his stress level became elevated by his pain or muscle spasms. He would lean on the "V" when he reached more than he could stand.

On the fifth day his doctors came in and asked Brock, "Do you want to go home?" This was the earliest they had ever had a Nuss Procedure patient go home. The normal stay is seven to ten days, and they were amazed that Brock had reached where he was in such a short period of time. We weren't surprised at all! God had his healing hand upon our son, and when God is doing the healing, the normal rules just don't apply.

The ride home was a difficult one. I understood more than most how every bump in the road is felt deep in the body. Try as I might, I couldn't avoid them all and at the end of the day I'm not sure which one of us was happier to finally get out of the car; Brock or me.

For the next six weeks our son had to sleep in a recliner or otherwise sitting up. He would not be allowed to lie down on his back or on his side till they were sure that the bar was safely and firmly fixed within his chest. Nena and I took turns sleeping in a recliner that we had pulled up next to his. He needed help just to get up out of his chair because he could not use his arms to push up at all. He could not twist or turn for the entire six weeks. But he was home now, where we could watch over him. With all the love and care we could provide, we were able to watch our son emerge from the darkest storm he had ever encountered. He came out on the other side of that storm a stronger young man, with a better understanding of life and his ability to call on Jesus when he was weak and weary. For the next three years, Brock will live each day with that titanium bar surgically fixed inside his chest. But, in looking back he was an inspiration to all who witnessed what he went through, and I can say that because he's not just anyone; HE'S MY SON!

CHAPTER 5

The Song of My Life

I f I mention the song *"Ring of Fire"* to any country music fan, they could tell me that it was Johnny Cash who sang it. Mention, *"I Wanna Hold Your Hand"* to almost anyone on the face of the planet and they'd tell you it was the group known as the "Fab 4", The Beatles who sang it first. Some songs mark a singer for life. Marty Robins will always be synonymous with the song *"El Paso"*, just as *"Midnight Cry"* will always be attributed to Ivan Parker.

Many artists have taken a song and made it their own, but rarely does a song take an artist and make him its own. But this is what happened to me when I first heard "I'll Run with You". This song was not just a mirror to my past and a vision into my future but it was in all actuality, the song of *"my life."*

It started when *"Butch Cassidy and the Sundance Kid"* hit the road again. Actually it was Steve Oglesby and I and we were headed for Eufaula, Oklahoma. I'll leave it up to you, the reader, to decide which one of us is Cassidy and which one is Sundance! We've called ourselves that for years now but I don't think we even know which one of the two we are; but in my mind I think that I'm supposed to be the "good looking one."

We were on our way to a singing on a Saturday night with Bill Burns. Bill is best known for his mega-hit *"That's Him"* by the Hoppers. Other favorites that he has penned include *"Cry of His Child"*, *"Forever Settled"* and the recent Top 20 song *"On My Journey Home"* by the Old Time Gospel Hour Quartet. I was one of several guest singers that were scheduled to be at his place in downtown Eufaula that night. I was looking forward to meeting Mr. Burns. Being the great songwriter that he is, I hoped I might be able to pick up a few writing tips from him. And, in the best-case scenario, he might even have a song or two in his "quill" just for me. Either way, I had a feeling it was going to be a great event.

We all gathered that night in a non-descript, tucked-away furniture store in the beautiful town of Eufaula, Oklahoma. Seating for this affair basically goes like this: get there early and get a recliner or a sofa; show up late and you're banished to a breakfast table somewhere. Fortunately all the sofas and recliners are pointed in the same direction so none of us had to sing to the back of anyone's head.

One of the artists performing that night was a lovely lady by the name of Marlene Pelt. Not only did she have a beautiful voice but she was a very talented songwriter as well. She had won many awards for her vocals and writing, including being chosen as the "Pen Writer of the Year" in 2004 by the Branson Singer Songwriters Association. Marlene and her husband Tommy were a blessing to get to know that night and she would come to play a pivotal role in how *"I'll Run with You"* made its way to me.

I was the last artist to sing that Saturday night. Bill Burns had asked me to close the concert with my testimony. I shared how God had walked with me through my many physical storms and how I knew that there would come a day when I would be able to do in heaven what I'd never done on earth; that is to run. "Oh, I might limp up to the gate," I said, "but I knew I would be running on the other side."

At the conclusion of the evening, Marlene and Tommy Pelt made their way to speak to me. Marlene said, "I know I have heard a song that fits your testimony exactly." She could not remember at that time just who the song writer was, but she said, "I remember hearing it in Branson in 2004 at a song writers' convention." For a song to make an impact after only being heard once, and then for it to be so powerful that it is remembered four years later, well that's got to be some song, I thought. Marlene said she believed she had the songwriter's contact information somewhere at her home, and that she would try her best to get us together. "This song is *your* song," she said, "and you need to be doing it."

I have exchanged many business cards with people over the years and with good intentions to reconnect on both sides, though rarely does anyone ever follow up. But Marlene did; she was on a mission!

Three weeks had come and gone and I was honestly surprised when I checked my email one evening and found that Marlene had sent me the contact information on one of the two writers of I'll Run with You: Joey Kay. He and Paula Lett were the composers of the song and they lived in Pell City, Alabama. Paula was the pastor's wife and she also served as the Music Director at The Harvest Center Church in Pell City. Joey Kay played bass guitar in the praise team there, as well as being the audio engineer for the church.

Joey was sitting in church at a Sunday night service and just before Pastor Lett began to preach, Joey began to write. (He later apologized for not paying attention during the message, but told Pastor Lett about the song. He replied that he knew Joey was writing and that it was OK!) Joey's lyrics for the song revolved around one thought, those who serve the Lord "against the odds".

Joey was thinking about how all our "disabilities" will be left outside the gates of heaven when we get there, and even if we limped up to the gate, all of that would change once we stepped inside. Many serve the Lord "against the odds" without any outward signs of the struggle. But there are those that we see struggling to serve and it leaves us wondering, "How *do* they do it?"

If Joey would have had to take a test on the message that Pastor Lett preached that night, there is no way he could've passed. He didn't remember much about the message at all, but by the time church was over he had written the lyrics to the song; even the re-writing had been done. In looking at the lyrics he believed he held in his hand something special. But his words had no music, which was strange for Joey because he writes songs like I do, where the lyrics and music all arrive on the page at the same time.

After the service, Joey went up to Paula Lett and asked if she had a minute. He told her he had an inspiration for a song, and had penned some lyrics, and wanted to know if she could read over them and see if they might inspire a melody.

One of the members at the time at Harvest Center was a man by the name of Daniel Ray who was pursuing ministry through song, and was doing remarkably well considering he had cerebral palsy and suffered with a significant disability in his legs. Paula knew that Joey had penned the lyrics with Daniel Ray's struggles in mind.

Paula went to the keyboard and almost immediately a tune came to her mind and she began to play. They tweaked a couple of words here and there, added a few chords for the bridge, and it was done. Within an hour, they had completed a song that was very moving. They both left the church that night knowing that God had done something incredible; they just happened to be the pen and the piano He used to create it. They really had no idea what God would do with this song, but soon we would all see His plan play out with each and every time that song was sung.

After receiving an mp3 of the song from Joey Kay, and listening to its powerful message, I was sold. When I talked with Joey on the phone that day I told him that I really wanted to record their song. I said, "I know who you thought you wrote the song for, but I believe it was written just for me." Then I offered to send him a copy of my book "*Chasing the Wind*" *as proof.* "If, after reading the book, you don't feel like this is the song of "*my life*", then I won't record it," I said. That was the deal I made with them and I wouldn't go back on it. If Joey and Paula, after reading my book, didn't feel that the song was a mirror to what's found in my life's story, then I wouldn't pursue the matter any further.

It wasn't long after Joey received his copy of the book that he called me. Almost immediately after I said hello, Joey emphatically said, "The song is yours!"

The "mission" that Marlene Pelt had so diligently pursued was now complete. This song that had touched my soul and claimed me as its own would soon come from my lips; and I could only pray that God would use it to reach the souls of others.

Shortly after recording *"I'll Run with You,"* I was back on the road again doing solo concerts on the days that Southern Grace had off. One day, Steve and I were headed to Missouri for a Sunday morning concert at Brighton Highway Assembly Of God, located just north of Springfield.

This was one of the longest drives I had made in the past few years, and my legs we telling me about it. "Did you know it gets cold in Missouri?" My Aunt Shirley (my mother's sister) lived in Brighton at the time and she had told me before we headed out that way that it was cold. But I thought to myself, "She's talking to a self-proclaimed polar bear, so how cold could it be?" The answer, very cold!

One of the ladies in my Aunt Shirley's Sunday school class at Brighton Assembly took it upon herself to make the demanding task of traveling long distances for me, a little bit easier. Twyla Menzies was her name and her faith could move mountains almost as fast as she could talk. Just being in her presence could make you feel good about being alive and serving a loving God. It also could cause your brain to pull a few negative G's as you tried to keep up with any conversation you were having with her.

She believed with all her heart that I needed a van to travel in. With a van, as scary as the idea might seem, I could lie down in the back and leave the driving to "Butch, or Sundance". It didn't matter to me who was who as long as he was the one doing the driving and I was the one doing the resting.

Quicker than Twyla could say, *"Jesus Loves Me, This I Know,"* she and her husband Bruce located the perfect van. Through her "ministry fundraising" abilities, and along with the willingness of many special people who wanted to plant a seed of faith into my ministry, she raised the funds needed to purchase the "I'll Run with You" van. But how would I get the van from that small car lot in Springfield, Missouri to my driveway in Dallas? Wouldn't you know it; God had that worked out as well!

Twyla and Bruce were having dinner with two of their friends, Lona and David Walker from Joplin, Missouri. Lona Walker is a well-established singer/songwriter with many of her songs having been recorded by well knows Gospel artists. As they visited over dinner, Twyla shared with David how they had found and purchased a van for my ministry, but had no idea how they would deliver it to me. "Where does he live?" David asked. "In the Dallas area," Twyla replied. David then calmly said, "I travel to the Dallas Car Auction at least once a month and I pull a car hauler behind me when I go. I could just load the van up and take it straight to Boyd on my next trip to Dallas." Isn't it amazing how God always has a plan? It should be comforting to all of us to know that nothing ever *"just occurs"* to God!

God not only meets the needs of his children when they cry out to Him, but He preemptively moves the pieces into play that cover those unforeseen needs that haven't even arisen yet. This would become obvious to all of us in the Chisum household over the next twelve months, as God continued to strengthen our spiritual ties to an Alabama Connection.

We traveled across several states over the next year in the I'll Run With You van. I even had custom plates made for it that read "RUN W ME". Together, Steve and I were able to witness God's healing touch upon countless broken lives and all because a group of God's children were willing to step out and meet a need, so that the gospel of Christ could go forward into areas that they themselves could never go.

Over that year, Joey Kay and I became great friends. We spoke to each other almost every day. I made a trip to Pell City, Alabama to do a solo concert at The Harvest Center, and after witnessing the music ministry there first hand, I had a better understanding on how such an anointed song could come from two of its members. Paula Lett, Joey Kay and the rest of the praise team at Harvest Center wouldn't just sing a song of praise. Oh no, they would *"attack it"* with all the love and energy they had within them.

By the end of that year, Southern Grace's concert schedule had become increasingly hectic and unfortunately, because of that, the I'll Run With You van stayed parked in my driveway. I was spending more and more time riding "The Blue Goose" and as the weeks and months went by I began to feel guilty that such a special gift as my van was not being used. I prayed that God would find a way for this beautiful bequest to return to the role for which it was intended. I was both pleased and surprised to see what my Heavenly Father provided as an answer to that prayer.

God planted a thought in the back of my mind on that day that Joey Kay informed me he had been hitching a ride with a friend to and from work for almost a week. His wife Amy's car had "given up the ghost" so Joey had to give his truck to her so that she could get to work. This two-car family was now down to one and nothing short of a miracle or a new engine could save Joey from that always-uncomfortable feeling of having to depend on someone else to get him to and from his job in Birmingham. He asked if I would pray that God would provide a solution for him and his family. I told him I would certainly be in prayer. But, what I didn't say was that I was positive that that his prayer needs and my prayer needs had *both* just been met, by an all-knowing, merciful Father.

That night I discussed with Nena what God had laid on my heart, and after we had prayed about it, we both knew what we needed to do.

Joey Kay and his wife Amy were on a plane leaving the borders of the "Crimson Tide" and entering into God's Country; TEXAS. We had decided that since God had given to us (through the hands of His children) the I'll Run With van, that we couldn't take that gift and then turn around and take money for it by selling it. It had been a gift to us and it should remain a gift to someone else, someone who needed it and would use if for the glory of God. It is amazing how one of the co-writers of a song that the van was named after would now be coming to claim it just as I had over a year before. They would accept it as we had, as a blessing and an answer to prayer.

The weekend that we spent with Joey and Amy at our home in Dallas was filled with laughter, love, music and thanksgiving. When they left in the van, headed back to Alabama, I was proud to know that we had passed a blessing on to someone else and that in doing so they could continue to tell the story of *I'll Run With You.*

Somewhere today in the small town of Pell City, Alabama, there is a van. This van is either hauling kids to and from church or helping spread the gospel through a multitude of church ministries. If you look closely at the license plate, you will see that the personal plates I had made that read "RUN W ME" are gone now and Alabama plates have taken their place. But, I know that Joey and Amy understand that the power of the gift didn't come from us. The gift came from a Heavenly Father who moved all the pieces into play to meet a need long before it even occurred to any of us that there would ever be a need. If you ever run across a deep blue Dodge van with an Alabama license plate that reads "RUN W ME 2", well just wave and tell Joey and Amy that the Texas Connection says hello!

CHAPTER 6

Lacee's Story

(He Who Made the Tiger Also Made the Lamb)

L ittle Lacee Johnson blessed this world on October 23, 1982. I am sure she would have loved to have roared her existence into mankind, but the air she needed was not yet available to her. While her mother Lisa went through the panting process that a delivering mother knows all too well, her baby girl was being strangled by the lifeline that had sustained her for the past nine months. The roar of the tiger fell silent, for now.

Just how long this child had been without oxygen for was unknown. But the constriction by the umbilical cord around the neck of this 8 pound 1 ounce gift from God was obvious by her pale blue complexion. The delivering staff at County Hospital acted quickly but it was painfully clear the damage had been done. Her left arm was withdrawn and held tight against her chest, unmovable and fixed. It was the second sign of her fight for life in what is ironically called the birth canal. Lacee finally began to breathe and a new life had begun; a life that would touch and forever change all who came to know her.

Days later, Lisa would leave the hospital in Arlington, Texas, headed for the safety of her mom's in Indiana. It would be there that she hoped to discover the answers to the questions that were haunting her both day and night. The echo of the unknown would not go away. Why is it that her baby could not move her left arm? What else could have happened to her sweet little girl in those early moments of birth? But the tiger remained silent and hidden within that precious bundle she carried in her arms and so close to her heart. The same heart that soon would break from the answers she was now seeking.

Dr. Skidmore, Lisa's mom's primary care physician, painstakingly went about the process of examining Lacee. He was a good doctor, thorough and to the point. After the exam, Dr. Skidmore sat Lisa and her mother down and delivered the heartbreaking diagnosis of CP: Cerebral Palsy. CP is a condition, he explained, that takes place when the brain is starved for oxygen for too long. CP includes a variety of conditions, and is not an illness or disease itself. Instead, it is the description of a physical impairment that affects movement. No two people with CP are the same, and the degree to which it affects people varies from barely noticeable to extremely severe. Time would be the teller of how severely Lacee would be impaired.

Dr. Skidmore referred Lacee to Dr. Mann, who was practicing medicine back in Arlington, Texas. Doctor Mann subsequently sent

Lacee to, my home away from home, Scottish Rite Hospital for Children. It is a miracle, I believe, as I write this story now, to realize that the same surgeon, who watched over me, was now watching over a young child that I would one day write about, twenty-nine years later. God has always had a plan and I can't help but see His handiwork on display in the weaving of Lacee's story and mine. Lacee entered Scottish Rite Hospital at almost the same age as I did, but a decade after I had already gone.

The gentleness of the lamb was always present in Lacee as a child. Her sweet and soft demeanor and beautiful unashamed smile were not diminished by her disabilities. She was the light of whatever room she entered.

Lacee loved many things in her childhood: her mom, her big sister, Terra, and younger brother, Michael; but few compared to the love she had for her walker. It was her freedom in the form of wheels and hand rests that helped give her a sense of normalcy. The only thing that even came close was the all-electric, pink bike with the button on the right handle to make it go. And boy, did she ever make it go!

Lacee was four years old when she learned to walk. She was able to accomplish this amazing task only through the imagination and creativity of her loving mom. Lisa had found a little plastic shopping cart. As Lacee began to pull herself into a standing position with her good right arm, Lisa would fill that plastic shopping cart with books. The weight of it fully loaded offset any chance that Lacee's small frame would topple it over. The added weight also created resistance that would strengthen her weak little legs as she strained to move an inch or two and then a foot or three. Then, as Lacee gained strength, books were removed, one at a time, forcing her to work on her balance.

As the cart became easier to move, so did Lacee, until finally over time, there were no books, no cart, just Lacee. The chains of a captive's body were now set free. The day she showed off in front of her elementary school principle, Mr. Moor, and walked across the floor unassisted was the first time she would bring a grown man to tears. It would not be the last. The tiger within her was now on the move.

The Burleson Independent School District played an enormous roll in the growth of Lacee. They helped to provide physical therapy, occupational therapy and speech therapy over those most formative years. They truly went the extra mile to help provide walkers and wheelchairs, along with splints to help with Lacee's left "helper hand." Lacee would undergo many surgeries over the years on both legs with cast from toe to groin. When she could no longer fit into the school restrooms, due to her casts and wheelchair, she was home schooled. All of this enormous effort was made to help her feel accepted, equal and as normal and loved as any other, well bodied child could feel. It worked.

Terra is Lacee's big sister, although the "big" part of that description really only consisted of one year, one month and one day. They were really closer to being twins than just sisters. They shared and celebrated birthdays on the same day and often wore the same clothes and shared the same bedroom. It was a room where they held countless tea parties, played with their "Barbies" for hours, and progressed over the years to deep, private conversations, the kind that only the closest of sisters can have. Together they created worlds of their own.

Terra watched as her little sister struggled to break free from the walls of her physical confinement as well. Dozens of surgeries on almost every body part with long recovery times and constant pain, all made an impact on Terra. She was amazed at the quiet strength that lay just under the surface of her little sister's small and tortured frame. But even when half of her beautiful hair was shaved off or when both legs were in casts,

Lacee never complained or took her pain out on anyone. She was, and still is, the strongest person Terra has ever known.

Maybe images of that strength could be found on the walls of Lacee and Terra's room. On each wall were beautiful posters of what Lacee loved so much, her tigers. One tiger in particular symbolized to Terra that internal strength that flowed so freely in the veins of Lacee. It was the picture of a young tiger resting its head upon its paw. There was something about its eyes. The tiger looks calm and content but there is a quiet strength in its eyes that makes you aware of its incredible power. Yes, it was a mirrored reflection of Lacee.

Michael is Lacee's younger brother. Living in a house full of estrogen was not easy at times but Michael made the best of it. Unfortunately, he also made the worst of it. He also thrived at being a tough little boy and was not always the kindest of brothers. I'm not sure brothers and sisters are supposed to mix well in their younger years. "Sugar and spice and everything nice" never mixes well with "frogs and snails and puppy dog tails". However, there was a day of reckoning coming. The tiger had been played with enough and when she would finally strike, Michael's life would never be the same again.

The day of comeuppance was nothing out of the ordinary. There was no foretelling or obvious clue that Lacee had reached the end of her patience with her tormenting younger sibling. But she had had enough; and Michael was about to be informed of it.

Michael was naïve. He did not understand how and why Lacee was different. In the midst of being tormented on this day, Lacee grabbed Michael and shoved him into the bathroom, followed in after him and quickly locked the door behind her. Slowly she turned to face Michael and through her tears and in the midst of her screams, she began to slap him again and again. She screamed out how awful he had been to her. How he was supposed to love her and not be cruel to her, and that she had had enough and from this point forward things would change. With each stinging slap the realization of what he had done, how he had been, came crushing in on him. Tears began to flow down his burning cheeks as he cried for forgiveness. Together in that locked bathroom, Michael and Lacee came to a new understanding. They turned a page in their relationship that afternoon. The thorn in the tiger's paw had been sufficiently removed. When the bathroom door was once again unlocked, so was a better understanding of Lacee for Michael, along with a new unbreakable bond between them both.

From that moment on, Lacee became Michael's best friend. Lacee would eventually confide in Michael about those children at school who were being cruel to her. Maybe it was his firsthand knowledge of how such tormenting was hurtful to her that caused him to want to rush off to school and confront those bullies all by himself. This time it would be he who wanted to give a "one-on-one" bathroom teaching session. Lacee would have none of it. She was emotionally revived just in the act of unloading her pain. No further action was needed.

Lisa had been a member of Praise Temple, a local church where all three of her children had grown up. Lacee, Michael and Terra all had come to know Christ and were baptized at this loving church. Lisa thrived with this band of believers and became the church secretary and taught Children's Church. She also took on the responsibilities of being the head of their Missionettes Ministry. With all this, it is no wonder that Lisa had no idea what was formulating and fermenting in the minds of those scheming youth at Praise Temple. Because of her responsibilities, she was seldom able to be in the sanctuary on Sunday morning, but if she had been, she might have been forewarned or at least been able to see the weaving of a plan so unpredictable, so calculating, so top secret, that no one above the age of eighteen had clearance to know of it.

Larry McDowell was the drummer for the praise team at Praise Temple. The youth had decided they would make it their mission to get Larry and Lisa together. In the book of Genesis, God said, *"It is not good for man to be alone. I will make a helper suitable for him."* The youth at Praise Temple thought Lisa was more than suitable for Larry; she was absolutely perfect. Their plan came together, and so did Larry and Lisa, as they were married in 2001.

The caliber of man that Larry was, and is, can be seen plainly in the courage and depth of love that it took for a single man to take on a ready-made family of four. The puzzle of life, with all its missing and sometimes ill-fitting pieces, had finally come together for all of them. It revealed a picture that each had longed for and needed to see, the picture of a loving family.

Lacee graduated from high school in 2002. With Larry, Lisa, Michael and Terra all looking on, Lacee boldly, but with great effort, walked across the stage without her walker to shake the Principal's hand and receive the recognition of a job well done. Proudly she stood with diploma in hand, signifying to all who were there, "I did it!" It was a day that honored not only her but so many of those "behind the scenes" individuals who gave Lacee so much in order that she might grow, thrive and contribute.

By this time in her life, her sister Terra had already started college at Texas A&M University. It wasn't long until Lacee joined her. Lacee wasn't eligible to enroll as a student on campus, but she wanted to experience college life more than anything, so Terra asked her to move in with her at College Station. For one great year they encountered all that life had to offer, wide-eyed and unafraid and most importantly, together. In all accounts, it just might have been the greatest year of Lacee's life.

After that wonderful year at A&M, Lacee moved back home with Lisa and Larry. Finding a job was very hard for Lacee. There seemed to be no one who wanted to take on an employee with Lacee's disabilities. She eventually, and to the betterment of all I might add, went to work with her mom at the local school, helping teachers and students alike for three days a week. The number of lives that she was continuing to touch was quickly becoming immense and incalculable.

One of the great joys that Lacee and Terra enjoyed was the time they shared over their often-impromptu lunch dates. Those special moments continued even after Lacee had returned home. These were unforgettable times, where they could talk about anything and everything. It gave Terra the feeling of being that "big sister" once again.

On those sunny days where she just couldn't stand to stay cooped up in the office and the thought of working one more second was more then she could bear, Terra would always find a way to leave and pick Lacee up for lunch and maybe go see a movie. It was an attempt at one of those spur-of-the-moment lunches when things drastically began to go wrong.

Lacee had been suffering from terrible headaches and neck pain for a couple of weeks. They became so severe that she had to be placed on medication just to get through the day. It was unsure if it was the pain from the headaches, the medication she was taking for it or a combination of the two that had left Lacee lethargic and groggy. Just how bad it had gotten was soon to be discovered.

Terra was in the process of moving from a home just a few houses down from Lacee to a new place in an adjoining town. Terra decided to go by and take Lacee out and see if the outing might make her feel better.

She could get back to the process of moving after she had checked on her sister, she thought. It was then that a series of strange events started to unfold.

Terra would normally just use her key to open the door at her mom's house, but on this day she had left that key behind so she knocked on the door and waited for Lacee to open it. In Lacee's attempt to get to the door, somehow she fell. After what seemed like forever Lacee was able to open the door, but it was more than obvious to Terra that something was wrong. Lacee seemed somewhat confused and still lying on the floor. Terra quickly called to her mom at work, and she immediately came home.

When Lisa arrived she found Lacee still disoriented and sitting in her chair. At first Lisa and Terra both thought maybe Lacee had just taken too much of her medication. Lacee said she was hungry so Lisa went to the Dairy Queen to get her something to eat. After eating, Terra made the suggestion that a shower might make her feel better, but Lacee was having none of it. All Lacee wanted to do was sleep. Maybe sleeping the medication off was a good idea, they thought, so they helped Lacee into bed. Barely five minutes had passed before Lacee began to beat on the wall, trying to get someone's attention. She needed help in getting to the bathroom. As Lisa lifted her to her feet, Lacee's knees buckled beneath her, and it was at that very moment that most believe Lacee suffered a stroke.

It didn't take long after the 911 call for the ambulance to arrive. By then, Lacee could barely talk and when she did it was unintelligible. After a short exam at the hospital in Huguley it became clear that Lacee's needs exceeded this facilities' capability and she was sent by ambulance to Harris Methodist Hospital in downtown Fort Worth.

Waiting for the ER Department at Harris Methodist to find a room for Lacee, Terra convinced the rest of her family to go and get some rest.

It was well past 2:00 AM at this point and the entire family was both physically and emotionally drained. They would need all the strength they could muster when the MRI, CAT scan and blood test results came back the next day.

In the meantime, Lacee was temporarily moved into a secluded area of the ER. It was a blessing just being "tucked away and out of the way" thought Terra from the hectic pace of a big city Emergency Room.

Lacee had become more coherent since arriving at Harris Methodist, and she began to ask for pain medication to help her cope. After checking with the attending physician, a nurse returned with a syringe filled with her much needed relief. Lacee's blood pressure, pulse and oxygen saturation levels were all being electronically monitored. These monitors are often fickle and the mere movement of an arm or shifting of your body would set off alarms. These alarms would go on and off so frequently throughout the night, it was impossible to get any rest and it also had the unattended effect of "crying wolf". Because of their secluded location in the ER, those alarms were also hardly audible to the nursing staff and with each annoying beep, Terra would have to find a nurse to check it out and ultimately punch the reset button.

After several hours of this, Terra's nerves had reached their breaking point. In the midst of all this uncertainty and chaos, it was always Lacee's sweet voice that calmed and soothed each irritation. Sleep finally came for Lacee and Terra but it was a fragile, exhaustive sleep, that didn't last for very long.

Terra was once again startled by the sound of alarms going off. In that fog induced haze that comes with very little sleep, it took a moment to realize that this time the alarm was different. Franticly, Terra went searching for a nurse. This time it was the real deal and the alarms were indicating a significant drop in Lacee's blood pressure. Maybe the drop in blood pressure could be attributed to the administering of the pain medication, the nurse suggested, more to herself than anyone else, but this was a significant problem that needed to be dealt with immediately.

As the nurse wheeled Lacee back into the main part of the emergency room, Terra quickly asked, "Do I need to call my mom?" The reply from the nurse didn't seem to answer the question as she simply responded, "Everything is fine." Her actions, however, were sending a signal to Terra that everything was not fine. Within minutes, in the midst of utter horror and disbelief, Terra would hear that same nurse ask if she would like a Chaplain to be called. And with the faint answer of "Yes," the curtain to Lacee's room was then quickly closed like an exclamation mark of the impending finality to the longest night of her life.

With the entire family now present and huddled together, they braced themselves for the oncoming storm. The emergency room physician had joined them in this small counseling room and in a monotone voice he said, "Lacee has slipped into a coma."

Lacee was soon intubated and placed on a ventilator to help her breath. She was also moved to the Neuro Intensive Care Unit, as they waited for the results from the tests done the night before to come in. Maybe this would shed some light on Lacee's sudden decline. After review of the MRI and CAT scan they believe they had found a piece of the puzzle. The diagnosis was Chiari Malformation.

This condition is basically a boney malformation at the base of the skull that places pressure on the brain stem. This protrusion usually can't be seen by the naked eye and in fact it takes only millimeters of boney growth to cause symptoms ranging from terrible headaches, along with unyielding tension in the back of the neck, to fatigue and in the most severe cases disruptions in the spinal canal, and death. Lacee was scheduled for emergency surgery on Sunday afternoon to remove the extra bone growth and hopefully save her life.

The surgery went well, but Lacee remained in a coma. Lacee would show signs of consciousness from time to time. She would flutter her beautiful eyelashes whenever Michael or Terra would speak to her. This only raised the hopes that all was going to be fine. Every twitch or movement meant something and was seized upon as a sign of hope. Just a couple more days, they thought, that is all Lacee needs, and then she'll come back to us. It was so hard for the family to see her in this condition with half of her beautiful hair shaved off and tubes and monitors everywhere. Oh, how they longed to see the gaze of the tiger or hear the unmistakable laughter of the lamb.

By Wednesday, Terra began to have the awful feeling that Lacee would never regain consciousness. The realization was both heartbreaking and comforting all at the same time.

Finding herself at one point the only person in Lacee's room, Terra had something she needed to say to Lacee. Something she desperately needed to get off her chest. She had been tormented over what had happened on Friday night while she had stayed with Lacee, just before her blood pressure plummeted. Terra's heart was breaking because she had become so angry over all the alarms going off that night. She felt guilty and ashamed in the anger she had shown over not getting any sleep. It was the last emotion Lacee had seen from her big sister and now Terra was racked with guilt. She was in the process of holding Lacee's hand and telling her how sorry she was, when Terra caught a vision from the corner of the room. It was an apparition of Lacee with an angel on either side. She looked beautiful standing there so tall and happy. Terra knew then that not only was her little twin never going to wake up, but in fact she was already gone.

Did God allow Terra to see this vision in order to ease her guilt? I believe He did. I also think it was Lacee's way of giving the family the strength that they would so desperately need for what was about to happen.

Lisa and the rest of the family were in the hospital cafeteria having lunch when a phone call came requesting them to return to Lacee's room. Upon arrival they learned that the third MRI showed that Lacee had no brain activity at all. Lacee's doctor suggested that by Friday they should consider removing Lacee from life support. Lisa and Larry were numb and the words just seemed to echo in their ears. After gathering up the family they went to the only place of comfort they could think of: their church. There they would "hide themselves in the cleft of the Rock" and pray for God's will and for an anointing upon them of His sustaining and sufficient grace.

Many phone calls would need to be made before Friday. Friends and family would instantly set aside their needs and focus on the needs of a small few. They would drive countless hours or spend finances they didn't have, to say goodbye to one who touched their lives in such a profound and lasting way. Lisa's brother John and wife Jolene left Illinois for Texas as soon as they heard of Lacee's condition. Nothing would keep them from showing and sharing their love for Lacee. Not even two days' notice and over a thousand miles could keep them from her bedside.

Peggy Barnes, a close friend of Lisa's, skillfully and carefully broached the subject of designating Lacee as an organ donor. Lacee had touched and helped so many in her twenty-seven years of life, and now she could continue to do that very thing after death. Lacee was now a broken clay vessel whose healed spirit had taken flight for its heavenly home. The vision Terra had seen without a doubt proved that. Lacee was now running in heaven and she had no further use of walkers, wheelchairs or anything else for that matter that she had left behind.

On Friday the family gathered around the bedside of a loving daughter, a precious sister and priceless friend, and said their goodbyes. When all life support was removed, the Tiger and the Lamb were free.

The tiger represents the fight and fire of life that God placed in the heart of Lacee. The lamb is the gentle yet disabled body that God would use to bring amazing love to all who knew her.

HE WHO MADE THE TIGER ALSO MADE THE LAMB

I have shared the powerful story of Lacee with you so that you might better understand what follows.

~

Southern Grace and I were in the small town of Joshua, Texas in 2009. It was the size of town that if you blinked only once you just might miss seeing both city limit signs. But it was the size of the hearts of the members of Crossroads Fellowship in Joshua that really stood out. One in particular stood out above the others to me and that was the servant's heart of the man who had brought us there, Earl West.

We were so excited on this trip because we had on the tour bus with us, all the way from Pell City Alabama, Joey Kay. Joey was a co-writer of the song we were now using to close our concerts. A song that we were just beginning to see had God's anointing all over it. It is the song that I claim as "my song", the story of my life, and God's miraculous work in it. We had no idea when we sang *"I'll Run With You"* that day, how God would use this song through a servant's heart, to heal a whole family's broken heart.

Earl West approached me after the concert and told me briefly about a young lady he knew who had recently lost her daughter. This child had much in common with my story and "my song" because she had suffered from a disability all her life, Cerebral Palsy, and now she was running in heaven. Earl wanted to get a copy of *"I'll Run With You"* in order that he might share its obvious anointed message with this hurting family. Without hesitation, I placed a CD in his hands and left the results in God's.

The first time Lisa listened to *"I'll Run With You"* after having received it from Earl, she cried uncontrollably. She could not understand in her grief, why a friend would give her a song that talked about running when her Lacee had never been able to run. Why would he choose this song to try and comfort me, she wondered? He could never know how much it hurt to listen to the message of this song. So, after listening to it only once, she put the CD away, never intending to hear it again.

Lisa had stopped going to church, and was on depression medication. She had withdrawn from family and friends and had even refused to celebrate any and all holidays. She had lost herself amongst her countless tears and could not see past her deep sorrow and inconsolable loss. Little did Lisa know that God had a plan! God has always had a plan.

This CD that Lisa thought she had put away mysteriously kept showing up. Lisa would open a drawer or cabinet, throw it in and sure enough it wouldn't be long and it would be out again for her to find. Nothing is as persistent and unrelenting as the comforting will of God. And Lisa was learning that lesson first hand even if she didn't want to.

Finally that night Lisa gave in. "God if you want me to listen to this, then there must be something I need to hear," she said. And with that, she sat down and listened and through her tears God began to soothe, comfort and heal.

Lisa began to realize that she was missing Lacee so much that she couldn't see that Lacee was happier now then she ever could have been on earth. Lacee was home with God, in no pain and had no physical restrictions. For all eternity there would be no more stumbles, no more falling down. Lisa finally understood that the cruel stares of the uneducated that had tormented Lacee all her life were now replaced with loving looks from Love itself, Jesus Christ. This revelation changed Lisa in an instant and eventually touched, healed and changed the lives of Terra, Michael and Larry as well.

One of my greatest joys was looking out on the front row of a concert in late 2010, and seeing Lisa, Larry, Michael and Terra. I know without a doubt that night as I sang *"I'll Run With You"* that somewhere in Heaven, Lacee was running to see her best friend, Jesus.

CHAPTER 7

Grace Runs Deep

H ave you been *"Graced"*? That catchy phrase was first spoken by my good friend and the co-writer of *"No Time Today"*, Wanda Anderson Pearson. Southern Grace was busy traveling across Texas, Oklahoma, Arkansas, Kansas, and Mississippi asking the very question that she posed, to countless churches and individuals. We went out across this vast country with a mission to remind the "churched" that God's Grace is sufficient, and to inform the "un-churched" that His saving grace is everlasting, amazing and eternally transforming.

There are so many stories I could share with you about the lives we saw being changed. Trying to write it all here would be impossible. I am reminded of an old hymn written by Frederick M. Lehman called *"The*

Love of God". Originally there were only two verses to this song until a third verse was found penciled on the wall in a narrow room of an insane asylum, by a man who was said to be demented. These words were not found until the day the man died and a copy of what he had written was placed into his casket. It is this verse from a composer known only as "anonymous" that explains why it's impossible to share all of what God allows our eyes to see and souls to experience.

V. 3

Could we with ink the ocean fill,
And were the skies of parchment made,
Were every stalk on earth a quill,
And every man a scribe by trade;
To write the love, of God above
Would drain the ocean dry;
Nor could the scroll contain the whole,
Though stretched from sky to sky.
Chorus:
Oh, love of God, how rich and pure
How measureless and strong
It shall forever more endure
The saints' and angels' song

Even a demented man in an insane asylum, found implanted deep within his soul the knowledge of God's Greatness and the futility of trying to describe the depth of His love. As impossible as it is to do, I will attempt in this chapter, to share with you the full blessings of a loving God and somehow measure the depth of His grace; because I, along with the men of Southern Grace, have seen firsthand how "His Grace Runs Deep!"

The "Blue Goose" was flying south for concerts in Hallettsville, Texas on Saturday Night then on to Pearsall, Texas for another concert that following Sunday morning. It was cold and rainy on that second weekend of October 2009 but I was excited to be headed back to South Texas, where so many memories of my teenage years originate from.

Saturday night's concert in Hallettsville went well, although the attendance was down due to the fact that their High School basketball team, the "Brahmas", was playing in the State playoffs. Sure wish we had known that before we booked the concert because there were certainly a couple of long-legged members of Southern Grace who would have loved to have been there to watch the game themselves. But, even with a small crowd we had a great timesharing God's message of grace.

While in Hallettsville I had the chance to see my old friends, back from my high school days, John and Cindy Thompson. John and Cindy both knew how deep God's Grace ran, because it had sustained them through the storm of John's brain cancer and then delivered them safely to the other side of that storm. Any opportunity to spend time with a walking, talking miracle is humbling, and it is time well spent.

We left Hallettsville immediately after the concert, headed for San Antonio. The term "immediately" is somewhat misleading however because there is always an hour or so of tearing down and reloading that has to be done. Most people have no idea how much work is involved just getting there and getting set up for a one and a half hour concert. That's why the term "get a real job" is always laughable to anyone who tours in the music industry. Trust me when I tell you, it is a job just making it look effortless!

Southern Grace would spend the night in San Antonio before heading on further south to Pearsall, Texas for our Sunday morning service. Because we travel mostly on weekends, the time always seems to go by like a whirlwind. Just getting there and then getting all of us back home safely has often proved to be an adventure in itself, not to mention a test of faith and patience. The "Skipper" of the Blue Goose, Al LaConey, worked tirelessly to keep that bus headed down the road. But, I want to tell you, when you run the rubber off of a tire, early on Sunday morning, in the middle of nowhere and surrounded by cactus and mesquite trees; well you don't need the "Skipper" to tell you you've got a problem!

Our contact person for the concert in Pearsall was a young man by the name of Matt Fitch. He was the husband of a friend of mine. His wife and I go all the way back to my high school days. Now I must say in her defense that Sheiladawn Fitch was barely out of middle school back when I was a senior, but together we sang songs with all the youth of our church on our summer trips to church camp. Some of those songs I sang had a lasting memory with Sheiladawn, and because of that she persuaded Matt to help put this concert together.

I put in a call to Matt and told him we had a problem and that we might not make it in to Pearsall on time. He told us to come on anyway, take our time, be safe and he would find a tire for the Blue Goose when we arrived. True to his word, when we pulled into the church parking lot, Matt had made a call and found us the tire we needed. He also had talked the owner of the tire store into coming in on a Sunday (a day that he is normally closed) just for us. We quickly unloaded our equipment, and then Big Al took off with the bus, headed to the tire store. God used Matt to help meet the ministry needs of six guys he had never met, but whose hearts and souls were all connected to the same "Father."

This concert in Pearsall was a special event for me. I would have a chance to see friends and loved ones that I had not laid eyes on for more than thirty years. In the audience that morning, along with Sheiladawn and Matt, there would be the Dickeys, Jon and Linda Speed and the entire Dunkin family. I was so excited to be home, back in South Texas, and nothing could break or dampen my spirit that morning, not even a shredded bus tire or a cold drizzly October day.

This concert was an opportunity to show those that I had known years ago, that if God could change me He could change anyone. The last time I had been back in this part of the country I was touring in country music, deep in a life style that glorified no one but me. Now I was eager to share God's sufficient grace with my old and new friends alike.

Oh what a time we had that Sunday! The Holy Spirit moved across those who were there that morning like a cool refreshing wind. Before the day had ended, I had the privilege of leading a dear friend of mine from my childhood in the "*Believer's Prayer*". I want to thank you Lord for using us that morning to feed a lost, hungry world the *"BREAD OF LIFE"*.

Now, not all of our experiences together on the road have such deep spiritual meaning. Some of them are just fun filled and downright hilarious. Having a member of Southern Grace with a personality that rests somewhere between Ray Stevens and the Three Stooges makes life interesting. And, the term "interesting" certainly fits Roy Dale to a tee.

There were times I would step off the bus having no idea how I was going to sing because my ribs and stomach were so sore from laughing from the previous two hours of RD antics. I've heard it said that music calms the savage beast, but it is laughter that turns the light on in the beast's cage and brings him out of the dark. Walking shoulder to shoulder with Roy Dale, one will always find him or herself standing in that light!

The sun was shining bright the afternoon Southern Grace pulled into Round Rock, Texas. We were scheduled for a night concert at St. Philips

United Methodist Church and due to the "Skippers" lead foot we arrived a few minutes earlier then than we were supposed to.

Brother Dale Schultz, the pastor at St. Philips was scheduled to meet us at their Family Life Center, which was located in the middle of the church's vast campus. We were early for our arranged "load-in" and since the front doors were locked, Roy Dale went searching for any alternative entrance.

While most of us were busy out in the church parking lot, stretching the kinks of the road from our bodies, Joe Ayers decided to see what he could see through the glazed glass of the Family Life Center's locked front doors. The sun was so bright he had to cup his hands on the sides of his temples to help block the glare from the glass. He just wanted a "sneak peek" at what the inside of the building looked like, but he was not prepared for what he saw.

While we were busy stretching, Roy Dale had gained entry into the building and was even now waiting quietly, just on the other side of the same door that Joe was getting ready to peer into. Roy Dale had himself, just moments before, peered through the same door and had a good idea what Joe was getting ready to do. He would have to time his movements just right in order to get the maximum effect from what he was about to do. As Joe cupped his hands and strained to see through the glass, Roy Dale did the very same thing. They were face-to-face, eyeball-to-eyeball, with only a thin layer of glazed glass between them. I don't know what Joe expected to see, but I'm pretty sure it wasn't Roy Dale's "bug eyes and Cheshire grin"! Joe let out a yell like something had a hold of him, jumped back and then did his best impression of Peter walking on the water. We laughed till tears were rolling down our faces! Joe's heart may have skipped a beat or two, but even he saw the brilliance of Roy Dale's "perfect mime".

Roy Dale's humor has lifted the tired and weary bodies of Southern Grace on many different occasions and without his gift of humor, oh, we would still be doing God's work alright, but it just wouldn't be as much fun.

This is just a snapshot of our life on the road. We've laughed together, prayed together and we've cried together. The men of Southern Grace have stood side-by-side countless times and marveled at the moving of God's Holy Spirit in the lives of hurting individuals and longing congregations. God moves in and through the lives of His people and we have been blessed to be "a witness" to it all.

This last story of *"Life on the Road"* is about someone who knows the depth of God's grace. It is a story that I will take to glory with me because its sweetness and beauty is forever imprinted on my heart and in my mind. I know already that my feeble writing and less than perfect storytelling will not even come close to describing what went on that night at Austin Chapel Baptist Church; but this book would be incomplete if I didn't try my best to share it with you.

With the "Blue Goose" parked in the far corner of the Austin Chapel Baptist Church parking lot, we were inside and in a hurry! The evening concert was fast approaching and not all of us were dressed and ready to go. I had finished getting ready (or maybe I had just given up on what I had to work with) and I made my way to the front of the bus to allow more room for those still working on making themselves presentable. Looking out through the big front windshield of our tour bus, I could clearly see the crowd was already making their way into the church auditorium.

As I continued to watch the people of DeKalb, Texas and surrounding community's file in, my eyes were drawn to a woman with an obvious disability. I watched as she made her way with great difficulty across the paved parking lot. My eyes always seem to pick up on the slightest limp or physical problem that someone might be experiencing. I had seen it all in my lifetime when it came to physical limitations and because of that personal experience, very little escaped my view. This, that I was watching now however, was obvious, even to the untrained eye.

With both hands firmly fixed to her rolling walker, this woman seemed focused like a laser beam on her intended destination, even though I could tell her body seemed less dedicated in getting her there. Walking closely at her side and watching over her every step, was an elderly man. If I had to guess he had to be in his eighties and did not seem to be in great health himself. But, it was obvious that whatever health and energy he had left in his life, he was giving it to her.

I later learned that the old man shuffling close behind the woman on the walker was eighty-two year old George Jordan. He had dedicated the last fifty-four years of his life to taking care of his severely disabled daughter Myrtle, who was born with cerebral palsy on August 28, 1956. George's wife Gracie placed this tremendous weight of parental responsibility in his weak and wrinkled hands on January 23, 2009 when she left this world and went to be with the Lord.

It was George and Gracie Jordan who made sure their daughter Myrtle was raised in a Christian home and went to church regularly. They were there when Myrtle was saved back in 1965 at the age of nine and when she was baptized at Westwood Baptist Church in Houston, Texas. Those dates were permanently written down, not only in "The Lamb's Book of Life" but also in Myrtle's bible for all to see; and she would proudly show you even if you hadn't asked to see it. This is the same bible her daddy now carried for her as they entered Austin Chapel Baptist Church that Sunday night.

Myrtle has no way of communicating audibly with anyone. Oh, her utterances can be heard by those around her but deciphering the words locked away within her twisted and tormented body is impossible to do. Even after a lifetime with Myrtle, her father George often ends up playing a game of trial and error as he attempts to understand the needs and wants expressed by Myrtle. As frustrating as it is for her father and anyone else who encounters her, try to imagine if you can how maddening it is for Myrtle. She is smart, and knows what she wants to say and do, but her body holds her captive and will not let her go.

I was there that night with Southern Grace, to remind her that she would not always be held captive. One day she would throw away her walker, stand up straight, and run those streets of gold shouting words of praise that all of heaven would clearly understand. One Glorious Day!

Our concert started well that night, and when we had reached the middle of our service it was still going strong. But it was at the close of our concert, the point at which we sing *Beulah Land,* and *We Shall See Jesus,* that the Holy Spirit began to fall down like rain upon all who were there.

In the closing moments of the concert I began to share a portion of my testimony. I described how my old scarred up body would one day be changed in an instant to a glorified one, with no restrictions and pain free. I spoke of how long I have longed for that day, the day I would run those streets of gold. It was at this point that God delivered a spirit filled epiphany to Myrtle and she could no longer hold her excitement in. And it came pouring out like a river of rushing water.

As we began to sing the first chorus to *"I'll Run with You," "I may limp up to the gates but I'll run on the other side;"* Myrtle began to moan and cry out as she twisted and turned in her seat. *"And He will hold me in His arms and dry every tear I've cried."* Those around Myrtle began to cry, as they saw her spasmodic movements and heard her unintelligible utterances, as they seemed to crescendo with each line we sang. *"He'll watch me run those streets of gold when my body is made new."* Myrtle was getting a glimpse of her new body to come and everyone in church saw it too. *"I may limp up to the gates, but then I'll run with you."* She was ready to take off running right then and there if God would only have called her home.

Oh what a vision we all saw that night play out in front of our eyes. So many people get bogged down with the burdens of this world and forget that this is not our home. We really are just passing through! Myrtle, in her unique and special way, was reminding each of us to let go of this temporary world and fix our minds on the eternal life yet to come.

Just as the composer to the third verse of that old hymn was locked away in a dark, damp and dingy insane asylum, Myrtle too was locked away in her own cell; but her cell was her body. But in the end, they both understood who held the keys to their freedom.

We saw that night, in the life of Myrtle Jordan, that God's sustaining and eternally transforming grace will indeed one day bring freedom. And that Freedom is available to all who will claim it. Don't be afraid because you think your situation has become unfathomable, or you feel unreachable in the depths of where you are, because Myrtle's life stands as a living testament to the fact that *God's Grace Runs Deep.*

CHAPTER 8

Don't Let Being Good Keep You from Being Great

Music always came easy for me. Genetics, coupled with God's gift, made singing and playing music as effortless for me as breathing. That graceful gift of music has also been given to my son Brock. I began to see his talent come to the surface when he was nine years old, as together we recorded the song, *"That's What Fathers Do"*. His pure tone and almost perfect pitch gave those with a trained ear, early insights as to what would most assuredly come with age and maturity.

In middle school Brock excelled in both choir and band and over those two years, he began to make a name for himself. In the seventh grade Brock received a #1 rating (which is a superior rating) in Band UIL Ensemble and a #1 rating in Band Solo. He was nominated to All City Choir and received a superior rating of #1 in his UIL Vocal Solo.

In the eighth grade he turned it up another notch; he was chosen to be a member of the All Region Boys Choir. Here, Brock was awarded #1 rating in UIL Vocal Solo and was once again inducted into the ALL City Choir. At the end of his eighth grade year Brock was awarded the Choir Service Award; an honor given to only one student who exemplifies the true spirit of giving to others and mentorship.

Even with all of this success, Brock was still shy and reluctant to show the depth of his gifts. But, to those who were trained in the art of excavating hidden talent, the digging was already underway and it was beginning to unearth many beautiful gems.

The extent to which he was being noticed came into full view the day he went to freshman orientation at Poteet High School. He stood in line to meet his future choir director, Ms. Westgate. When it was his turn to step up and shake her hand, Brock started to introduce himself but she quickly and excitedly interrupted him and said, "I know who you are Brock, and I've been waiting on you for two years." Ms. Westgate had been watching him behind the scenes, waiting for the day she could help mold his God given talent. Brock was both surprised and honored that she had been watching him and her few simple words of encouragement made him want to prove her faith in him was justified.

As a freshman, Brock was chosen to be a member of the Varsity Choir. He was the only freshman in the past four years to have been chosen to sing with this elite choir. My son received # 1 ratings in UIL Vocal Solo as well as a # 1 rating in his Choir Vocal ensemble.

He played percussion in the Poteet Pirate High School Band and received a superior rating in his UIL Band Solo. He is an active member of this high school band; an award winning band that was busy setting records of its own. This band became 2010 Sweepstakes Band of the Year as well as Grand Champions in two of the biggest marching competitions in the State of Texas.

So you see, as a freshman, Brock was already racking up a tremendous number of gold medals and musical accolades. All of this was possible because our son was not just blessed with a God given talent for music, but because he recognized that gift and then with all of his heart he embraced God's plan for his life.

You might think that this chapter is all about a proud father who is excited about the accomplishments of his child, and it is. But it's not just about the pride of an earthly father, but more about the honor Brock brings to his Heavenly Father by using the gifts he's been given.

We all have gifts, talents, and skills that God has richly deposited inside of us for His glory. We don't need to hide our talents like the lazy servant in Matthew 25: 14-30, but draw them out of our hearts and minds, and bless others with them. God has great plans for our lives, if we will just believe and obey Him. *(Jeremiah 29: 11)*

We should daily whet our appetite for God. Develop a hunger for God and His presence. He is the one who gives us our gifts!

God wants to use you, but the bigger question here is, do you want to be used? Do you want an enriched, exciting life, living it to your fullest potential, or will you settle for a mediocre, boring existence?

Psalm 37: 4 says, "Delight yourself (take great pleasure) in the Lord, and He will give you the desires of your heart." What are your desires? Take them to Him, and then as you follow Christ, He will bring those things to pass!

Ask God, yourself, and others what your spiritual gifts, talents, and skills are. What are you really good at? Are you naturally good with computers and an excellent artist? Then you would probably be good as a graphic artist. When you speak at retreats, do you receive positive, encouraging feedback? Then you are skilled in communication. Your words have weight and authority, so use that gift to bless others. Do you feel deeply or cry when people are hurting, and try to comfort them? You probably have gifts of mercy and compassion.

The spiritual gifts can be found in *Ephesians 4: 11-12* (five-fold ministry gifts), *I Corinthians 12: 4-11* (manifestation gifts), and *I Corinthians 12: 28*. Find out what your spiritual gifts are, and begin to walk in that authority and anointing!

Tap into your creativity. Creative thought requires you to remain detached enough from any one idea to allow others to be considered. This may not come naturally to us, especially if we are used to censoring our ideas, as so many of us are. In other words, think outside the box. Allow your mind to go wild. Tell the critic living between your ears, to once and for all shut up, and then dare to believe what God believes; that you can be more than good with your gift, you can be great! I am not talking about being great in the eyes of the world, although that may happen, but more importantly about being great in the eyes of God.

Creativity requires that you give yourself permission to try new things and feel new sensations, like going on a hot air balloon ride in New Mexico, or skiing in Colorado. Be bold and don't be afraid to color outside the lines; use the big box of crayons with colors like Fuzzy Wuzzy Brown!

Exercise your gifts diligently. I know how muscles atrophy when they are not used regularly: "Use it or lose it." Do we really want to bury our talents for 40 years, and wake up one morning realizing we're old, it's too late, and we are not what we ever really wanted to be? Could I have been an artist, a singer, a soldier, a missionary in South Africa, a writer, a dolphin trainer? As we find out what our gifts, talents, and skills are, and begin cultivating them, they will flourish. Just like Brock, you too will see the rewards of using the talents God gave you and by doing so you will experience inner peace and happiness, along with bringing great joy to your Heavenly Father and to others.

The Lord gives us certain desires, for a good reason. Interestingly, these desires are often related to our spiritual gifts, talents, and skills, and ultimately to our calling. If you are just getting started in your craft, take steps of faith. Strive for excellence, not perfection.

Reach for your dreams. Be determined to live a full, beautiful life, and not waste a second. Life is just pregnant with possibilities and adventure!

One of my favorite movies is *"Secondhand Lions."* A young boy, whose mother abandoned him so that she could live a fun life, dropped him off at a strange house to live with his two old, grumpy uncles, who did not want him there. But eventually their relationship grew close, and he learned a lot from these larger-than-life men. One of the lines I love from the movie is after the uncles have died and left the nephew with all their inheritance (which was substantial). Telling another man about his two uncles, with great admiration the young boy said, "They really lived."

Are you really living? Are you alive in His Spirit or just existing in yours? Is this the life you really want? If it's not, then when are you going to start living?

Take the ceiling off your thinking. Loosen the limits you have conditioned yourself to that always surface from others' perceptions of you or from your own negative self-talk. Listen to what you tell yourself. Our thoughts have a great influence on our lives. Learn to train your mind to think positive thoughts of success, instead of poisonous, defeating thoughts. Latch onto a scripture such as, *"I can do all things through Christ Jesus who strengthens me!" (Philippians 4:13)*

What do you want to do? What do you love to do? Your passion is the key to understanding your gifts and abilities! I never feel more alive than when I'm singing or speaking in front of a large group of people. It used to scare me to death to stand in front of people and speak. I literally used to feel nauseated: as If I was going to faint. To be honest, I still get a little nervous just before singing or speaking, but as soon as I step up to the platform, it melts away as the anointing of God kicks in. Thank God for His grace and that precious anointing. I never want to do it without Him! And I LOVE it! I feel alive when I am singing, writing and speaking! It's the way God created me to be!

The Bible tells us we are to, *"Study to show thyself approved."* (2 Timothy 2: 15) This means to learn everything you can, to bring honor to God and to obey Him. Stay in God's Word daily. *Proverbs 4: 7* says, *"Wisdom is the principal thing; therefore, get wisdom. And in all your getting, get understanding."* Knowledge is worthless by itself unless you know how to apply it to your life. Find daily quiet time with God, and let Him speak to you and guide you. His Holy Spirit will teach you all things. *(1 John 2: 27)*

Pursue more education, classes, training, and seminars. Find a mentor to disciple you. Be like a sponge and soak up everything you can from people who are successful in your field of interest. How did they get started using their gifts or talents? What were the practical steps they took? Extract the precious from the worthless. God has a unique blueprint for your life that He wants to accomplish. It is He who is the "Master Mentor".

Our gifts are simply "special presents" from God that He eagerly waits for us to open. He has many beautiful surprises in store for us and others, as we seek His face. *"Unwrap The Gift"*, and then with gratitude enjoy it and use it for Him and to bless others.

Just as I started this chapter recounting and bragging on the accomplishments of my son, I want to end my life thinking that I have given my Heavenly Father ample reason to turn to all the saints and heavenly hosts and proudly say "Did you see what my child did with the gifts I gave him?"

So, what is it that God is calling you to do that is much bigger than you are? Nothing is impossible with God. And, He wants to do the impossible through you and for you! Don't settle for less than God has in store for you. Like the note my son has written on the mirror of his dresser says: *"Don't Let Being Good Keep You from Being Great"*, for the glory of God.

CHAPTER 9

A Burning Hope

The first time I laid eyes on Burning Hope it was on a hot sunny day in April. I would never be the same after that day. My eyes would be opened a little wider, my heart would love a little deeper and my life would forever be touched by the flame of "Burning Hope". As Steve Oglesby and I drove into the parking lot that day, we found the keeper of the flame to Burning Hope, dressed in overalls, wearing a baseball cap and straddling a riding lawnmower in the town of Trinity, Texas.

As we parked the car, we could see Burning Hope's pastor Jim Parrish, busy mowing the almost full acre lot that surrounded his church. As dust and grass clippings swirled up around his head and face he kept on mowing and simply waved as a signal to let us know he had seen us. We waited outside my car as Brother Jim made a couple more rounds before turning his undersized lawnmower in our direction.

As he turned the mower off the sudden silence was quickly broken by a booming country voice that said, "Hi, I'm Brother Jim and I'm a hugger." And with that, this large loving man wrapped his grass-laden arms around me and gave me the sweatiest, dust covered hug I've ever had. As I patted his back with my hand, he began to resemble the Peanuts Cartoon Character "Pig-Pen" as the dust flew into the air and swirled around him. His hug was both love filled and heart felt and I knew instantly that we were going to be great friends.

Over the next two days, Steve and I saw within the ministry of this small church, what so many other churches around this country seemed to be missing or somehow fail to do.

Burning Hope provides so many different avenues of outreach to the local community.

They "birthed" the local food pantry known as the Trinity Loaves and Fishes. This is a ministry that has now grown into an independent non-profit organization and is now fully supported by all the local churches and businesses and individuals alike. Even with that, Burning Hope decided to maintain its own small food pantry located at the church; a fail-safe if you will, just for those who stopped by the church and found themselves hungry and in need.

They also created a women's shelter called "The House of Hope" for those who were physically hurting from drug addiction or have been silently suffering through physical abuse.

The "Third Cross," a Christ-centered support group started by Burning Hope, reaches out to folks with drug and alcohol addictions as well as other life controlling issues and they meet to "touch a need" three times a week. These meetings are recognized by the State of Texas and can be attended instead of the local AA meetings. Local judges and law enforcement agencies have been known to bring folks to Brother Jim in lieu of locking them up. They're left in Jim's hands on the condition they cooperate as they go through the ministries that Burning Hope provides.

S.O.U.L. stands for Sharing Our Unconditional Love, and is Burning Hope's "Soup Kitchen" that feeds all the homeless in the area while giving them the opportunity to drink-in a taste of "The Living Water."

Anita once told me that, "I live all of this every day and even I find it sometimes hard to believe. Only God can do all this," she said, "because any sane person would know that mere human beings couldn't pull all of this off!" Yes, the faith of this little church is awesome to behold and it should be an example to us all.

Brother Jim and Anita are the "genuine, real deal". They don't just pass by in their car, honk and wave at those ugly hedges and byways; no, they get down in the mud and twigs and thorns, face to face with the hookers and drug addicts and they share God's love with them. Their motto at Burning Hope should be *"We don't care who you are or where you've been, come to Burning Hope and we'll love the hell right out of you."* Because you see, with the congregation at Burning Hope, that is exactly what they do every day!

The powerful little church actually started in the home of Burning Hope's first pastor, Kelly Adkins, in August 1994. After fourteen months the pastor left, leaving Jim and Anita to hold the congregation together while looking for a new pastor. They were the only ones there who knew anything about the administration aspects of a church. A foreign missionary, who was home on furlough, filled in as an interim preacher for four months and ultimately recommended that Jim become the pastor, as it was obvious to all that he and Anita were the "leaders" of the church. That foreign missionary took it upon himself to visit each member in their homes to get their opinions on his recommendation and, in the end, it was a unanimous vote; Jim and Anita were obviously "God's Anointed" for Burning Hope.

When their work first began in Trinity, there was resistance and from very unlikely places. Local residents made it a point to inform Brother Jim that Trinity, Texas wasn't in need of another church. After all, "this is just a small town," they would say, "and all the existing churches are already doing a more than adequate job touching lives for Christ." Oh really?

It was common knowledge in law enforcement circles that Trinity, Texas and its surrounding communities had often been referred to as the methamphetamine capital of the United States. Yes indeed, they didn't need another church in Trinity. What was needed, however, was a group of individuals that were sold out and turned on for Jesus Christ.

Trinity, Texas was desperately craving an outpouring of the Holy Trinity, through the heart and hands of loving people. People who were less concerned about the number of tattoos you had, the length of your hair, if you wore the right clothes or where you came from but were instead concerned about where you were going eternally.

There were those that told Brother Jim they were concerned that another church might just end up decreasing the number of existing flocks. Brother Jim tried to put those fears to rest when he boldly proclaimed; "I assure you, I'm not looking to steal members from any established church, I'm just looking for those individuals who might not feel welcome in those established churches."

God built Burning Hope through the hands of recovering drug addicts and ex-cons. The ministries flourished as recuperating alcoholics put down the bottle and picked up the Bible and went out and told a community of people that others had written off; that God loves them right where they are.

I've been in many churches across this country. I've heard preachers that spoke in melodic tones and others who spoke in tongues. I've been in churches where the congregation sits in the pews and others where they roll in the aisles. I've been in churches where people raise their hands in praise and others where they keep their hand on their wallet. I've been in everything from mega churches in Arizona to house churches in East Texas. In other words, I'm no stranger to church and from all I've seen, Burning Hope is getting it right. Now, is this church perfect? No! Burning Hope has issues just like any other church because its members are made up of fallible human beings. But, what separates them from most churches is in their ability to look through the eyes of Christ at some of this world's most unwanted and only see a precious saved soul in the making.

Brother Jim shared with us that there had been times over the years when individuals would walk, or should I say stumble, into Burning Hope under the influence of their chosen poison. It never took long after walking through the door for them to become sobered up and under the influence of something and "Somebody" more powerful than anything they had previously swallowed, shot up, snorted or smoked.

There was even a time during a tent revival on the river, where two old fishing buddies made their way into the tent for the free food and ended up staying for the service. They had been fishing all day, and from the way they were acting they had popped the top on their first beer the moment their first lure hit the water. When the music director of the revival invited those in the congregation who wanted to join the choir; they both decided they would try their hand at singing.

They made total fools of themselves, but Brother Jim refused any offers for them to be removed. Jim knew they would sober up soon enough and he had something to share that they needed to hear.

Sure enough by the time the music was over and the preaching started, the "good-old-boys" began to sober up, sit up, and take notice. When Jim Parrish closed the service and gave the invitation, both men couldn't hit their knees fast enough as they opened their hearts and accepted Christ as their personal Savior. These men didn't miss a single night of the rest of the revival, and they came sober and ready to worship.

Brother Jim went out of his way to make our first visit to Burning Hope a wonderful experience. That Sunday morning service was spectacular because the Holy Spirit showed up and showed out. Steve and I were blessed to have witnessed the Saving Grace of God in action that morning. In a time where so many of God's churches have begun to take a back seat to a secular world's agenda, it was refreshing to see God's power on display the "old school way"; through believers who truly believe and share with the lost and hurting an eternal burning hope.

I shared with you the story of Burning Hope because I truly believe that something is wrong in the Church today. I don't say that lightly, or as someone who thrives on criticizing everyone else so as to establish my own spiritual superiority, or as someone who is feeding on sour grapes because things aren't the way I would like them. I say it because of how many people I meet on a regular basis that are discouraged by traditional church and have chosen not to attend anymore.

Everywhere I turn, I hear people complaining about the same thing. This isn't something localized to a particular area, or limited to a certain social strata or denomination. I hear this from all sorts of people, many with impeccable spiritual credentials.

I often hear from pastors who have spent a lifetime in ministry and are now questioning the vibrancy of the Church. Others are just spiritual "newborns," armed with little more than a spiritual hunger, who refuse to attend church, not because they don't believe, but because they are repelled by what they see. Even those who have been a vital part of the church for decades seem to now be suffering from what I call "Stay Away Saint Syndrome."

No matter how you view this issue, no matter what position you have, no matter what church you belong to, you have to admit that something is wrong.

We are supposed to be the salt of the earth, as something that gives flavor to make a meal taste good. But when we are not attracting the lost, but rather repelling them, then our salt has lost its savor. What makes it even worse is that we are even repelling the saved.

There are opposing extremes to this issue, true, but shouldn't the middle be closer to the truth? We see on one hand the churches that are so "loose and loving" that they excuse any sin or misconduct, even accepting homosexuality and adultery in the church. On the other hand, there are those in their religious zeal that have taken it upon themselves to proclaim their self-righteous judgment on every church around them. Somewhere they have read that the Word of God is essentially a hammer that breaks 'the rock' into pieces, so in their misguided obedience they've traded in their fishing pole for a sledgehammer.

But in the middle of this spectrum, where one would hope to find something that is more balanced, instead we find a modern church that is socially based, smooth and sensual, sophisticated, and presented like a Hollywood production so that it will appeal to the crowds who flock there. Listen, if it walks like a duck, and quacks like a duck, and looks like a duck, then it most likely is a duck, and not a church.

And what, may I ask, ever happened to the Gospel of power? If our churches are supposed to be so good, then why are so many people turned off by them? If the fire that is burning in our churches originated from the altar of God, instead of a Wizard of Oz production, then I can guarantee you that hungry souls would be drawn by the Spirit of God; but instead they are turning away.

Where are the old-fashioned preachers who used to preach under the anointing of power, and relied not on their stack of glossy, graphically designed notes, but on the power of God to deliver the message? Many pastors today follow the social and marketing formulas they were taught in college and present a Gospel in a multi-media fashion with 7 bulleted points, a poem, and three jokes.

What happened to the strong calls for repentance that brought thousands down to the altar to repent and ask Jesus Christ to save their souls? This is the litmus test for Christianity. This is the essence of the Cross! The guidelines that the church of today seems to have forgotten can still be found in The Great Commission. If you are not winning souls, then you are a barren woman, and it is a shame unto you. Something is wrong!

Where is the outpouring of the Holy Ghost? Do we even know what it means anymore to feel the presence of the Spirit of God descend on a service and fill up the room with holiness? Or do we just think that our party atmosphere of excitement when someone plays a cool song or the excitement that we get when some charismatic speaker works up the crowd, is the Holy Ghost? Has it really been so long since we've seen the real thing that we don't even know what it is anymore?

Something of deep substance is missing in our church today. But we've become so sophisticated and enamored with our social gospel that we don't even realize that something is wrong. We are left like Gideon, threshing his wheat in secret by the winepress of God because our fields have been taken over by a worldly church. And we wonder out loud to the angel, "What happened to the miracles our fathers have told us about?" Yes, that's my question too: "what happened?"

I believe that when we, as God's children, lost our fear of God, we lost God's power in us. And at that point, as it says in *Isaiah 29,* the Book became sealed unto us so that we no longer even grasp how far we have fallen. We read it, but we can't see past the surface of the page.

The first step to real revival is to realize that we are in desperate need of one. Revival will continue to elude our churches unless, and until, we recognize that something is desperately wrong, and that we have lost something precious in our pursuit of a super-sophisticated, modern, 21st Century church. We've lost it, and we need to get it back.

2 Chronicles 7:14 is how we regain that which we've lost: *"If My people who are called by My name will humble themselves, and pray and seek My face, and turn from their wicked ways, then I will hear from heaven, and will forgive their sin and heal their land."*

I understand how in this chapter I might be coming off "a little preachy". But truthfully, my goal is simply to make this "a challenge chapter". A chapter to challenge today's body of Christ to **"Reignite Your Burning Hope!"**

CHAPTER 10

God's Poet

J ust outside of England's Sherwood Forest lives a man whose prayer can be poetry and whose poetry is but a prayer. He inhales the experiences of his life and exhales prolific words of beauty and grace; and all with a British accent! He is "God's Poet" and I am blessed to call Martin Holland my "brother and friend".

The one thing that all poets have in common is a passion for the written word. Martin Holland loves and lives the word, GOD'S Word! I have leaned on him in times of sadness and pain, and together we have shared moments of joy and celebration; but we have never actually met. Not once have we seen each other face to face, nor have we had the opportunity to collect on that long overdue hug. But being true friends doesn't happen because of one big thing; it happens because of a million little things. Distance and time cannot alter true friendship.

The Holland household consists of Martin, his lovely wife Linda and their two beautiful princesses, Rebekah and Rachael. I wasn't there physically for the birth of either of Martin and Linda's children, but my heart was. And I quickly saw photos in my "inbox" after each one blessed this world with their presence. Our friendship goes back over six years, and in that amount of time we have shared family secrets and celebrations, family needs and family sorrows. My household has truly been "grafted" to the British vine of Holland.

It was Martin's "mum", Beryl, known as "Granny B", who poured out her heart in prayer over a silk scarf that she would then send to my son Brock. That scarf was a gift, meant to heal and comfort on the day of his surgery and the long days that followed. Brock tied Granny B's beautiful silk scarf around the neck of his teddy bear and then he held it close to his chest during the many painful days after his surgery. Yes, our families are grafted together for sure; permanently attached at the heart.

Given the closeness of our two families, it is understandable that I would be concerned when Martin began to tell me how he and his family were being persecuted. A group of local thugs and misfits had begun to target Martin and his girls because they were different; because they were fighting for justice for the weakest members of society; because they were Christians.

In *Matt. 5:10-12* Jesus said; "Blessed are they which are persecuted for righteousness' sake: for theirs is the kingdom of heaven. Blessed are ye, when men shall revile you, and persecute you, and shall say all manner of evil against you falsely, for my sake. Rejoice, and be exceedingly glad: for great is your reward in heaven: for so persecuted they the prophets which were before you."

When we read verses like this it leaves us to wonder. And when we see good people suffer, we are tempted to doubt. When we ourselves experience trial and persecution in our own lives, we begin to question God; "Lord why do the righteous suffer, while the wicked prosper?"

I don't have a great answer for that, but I can tell you it has always been that way since the beginning and even until now!

Think about it. Abel was righteous and Cain was wicked. But as we know Cain killed Abel! David was said to be a man after God's own heart, so if that's true, then why is he constantly dodging the spears that were chucked at him? Why is Daniel, the purest in the kingdom, thrown into the lions' den? John the Baptist was referred to as the best man ever born of woman, and yet they beheaded him.

The Bible says, "All who live Godly in Christ Jesus shall suffer persecution! (2 Timothy 3:12) Note: it's not might suffer; it's SHALL!!!

Many years ago, when communism still held the Soviet Union in its iron clench, a little group of Christians met behind closed doors in the underground. This was a secret meeting of secret Christians in a church service that, for safety's sake, had to be secret.

Suddenly, the doors burst open, and two soldiers appeared with sub-machine guns. They shouted, "To all those who are willing to renounce Jesus Christ: you've got 5 minutes to leave! Everyone who remains will be shot immediately."

As you can imagine, every Christian in that place began to search their hearts and internally ask an important question; "Am I willing to die for Jesus Christ right now, today?" A few got up and ashamedly; quietly they left with their heads hung low. Most of the people stayed. As the last one left, a soldier shouted, "Is that it?" He held up his gun and repeated, "Anyone else?" Another man rose and ran out. The soldiers locked the doors, and turned toward the people that remained and then laid down their guns and said, "Brothers and Sisters, we too are Christians. We do not want to worship the Lord with anyone who is not willing to die for Him! Now that the half-hearted have gone, let's have church!"

Martin Holland and his family were not halfhearted. Although they had chance to move away from those who tormented them, they refused. You see, Martin and Linda had been witnessing to families around their block; one family in particular whose children often played with Martin's princesses. They believed with all their heart that God had placed them where they were in order to reach these families and bring them to the saving knowledge of Christ.

So they stayed, and in doing so their family would endure many hardships, including Martin being attacked in front of his heavily pregnant wife and 21-month old daughter, Rebekah. They then suffered the indignity of having a Police Sergeant phone the next day and gloat over having sent two of her officers round to 'rough up' Martin because "He deserved it"!

Their car would be vandalized repeatedly. Its tires were slashed, while its paint job was being ruined from the onslaught of eggs being thrown at it by those who Satan would use to try to stop God's work. And Martin has seen firsthand that "Truth and Justice" are sadly in short supply in the British legal and judicial systems!

If you live a life of faithfulness to the Lord as Martin and Linda try to do, and if you live a separated life, showing a distinct difference in Christ, and if you profess that Jesus Christ is Lord and that people need to be saved from their sins, you WILL suffer persecution. That is a promise.

Martin and Linda not only prayed for the souls of their tormenters, but they also prayed for a justice system that not only turned a blind eye to, but actively encouraged the harassment they were enduring. But as Martin says: "These are people who need Jesus, just like we all once did."

In *John15: 18-20* Jesus said, *"If the world hates you, you know that it hated ME before it hated you. If you were of the world, the world would love its own, but I chose you out of the world, therefore the world hates you. If they have persecuted ME, they will also persecute you."*

Perhaps the more searching question to ask is not, why do the righteous suffer, but rather ask, "Have I, as a Christian, ever been persecuted: and if not, why not?" Or, how long has it been? And if so, how did I respond? Did I rejoice when I was persecuted, as the Bible commands? Did I have a desire to retaliate, as the Bible forbids? Did I pray for those who persecuted me, as Martin and Linda did?

Have we become a world of "halfhearted Christians"? If our faith won't bring us back to God's house regularly, it is highly unlikely it would take us to the gas chamber. A faith that does not bring words of witness to your lips in our land of free speech would not likely go to a burning stake to be a public testimony for Christ. If our faith can't get the ten percent our Lord requires out of our pocket, I doubt it would get us to the chopping block for beheading! If our faith isn't strong enough to keep us away from worldly amusements and fleshly habits, it's not likely it would take you to the lions' den.

You can know for certain that you WILL NOT present yourself as a dying sacrifice if you aren't a living sacrifice *RIGHT NOW!*

I believe Martin and Linda would die for the cause of Christ. How do I know they would die for Christ? Well, for starters, it is plain to see that today, with all they have been through; they are a living sacrifice for Him right now!

Romans 12:1 "I beseech you therefore, brethren, by the mercies of God, that ye present your bodies a living sacrifice, holy, acceptable unto God, which is your reasonable service."

What is it we are willing to give for the cause of Christ? How out of "our comfort zone" are we willing to go? What pain are we willing to bear in order that we might do what God has called us to do? Are we sitting on our "blessed assurance" watching others do (with sometimes great physical difficulty) what we with well bodies could be doing? If you examine your Christian life right now, will you find it to be a halfhearted effort at best?

"God, forgive us today for having half-hearted devotion in light of the countless martyrs who've gone before us! Lord, help us to live for you, and if necessary, to die for you!"

P. S. ~ less than twenty-four hours prior to the writing of this postscript, Martin witnessed a portion of "The Harvest" from their years of planting. He was in church with one family from down the block, witnessing their four youngest daughters being baptized. Oh my brothers and sisters don't grow weary of the *planting*. If we are as faithful as "God's Poet", then we too will one day see a *Great Harvest*.

CHAPTER 11

Escaping Pandora's Box

At the end of each day, a veil of darkness will most assuredly fall. Before each of us closes our eyes to sleep, we will approach a corner that we cannot see around. That bend leads us to tomorrow. We are not promised the opportunity to turn that corner and even if we are so blessed, we cannot know what awaits us around that bend. Therefore, I could not have foreseen when I closed my eyes that Saturday night, June 26, 2010, the pain that lay waiting for me when the sun came up.

That Saturday afternoon we were busy packing equipment for the following day. I was booked to do the music and bring the message at

Faith Community Baptist Church in Maud, Texas. This was the church I had been ordained in and, as we packed, I began to get excited to see the friends and loved ones who would be worshiping there in just a matter of a few hours.

I had been hurting a little more than usual since a "rolling chair rodeo" episode backstage at Will Rogers Coliseum, two weeks earlier. But I had not given much thought to how sore I was and that the soreness had not yet gone away; I just kept on moving and tried to ignore it.

I don't know why I feel funny about sharing with you my strange sleeping habits, given all you already know about my life from my preceding book and the earlier chapters of this one; but I do. Of course, that won't keep me from telling you that I rarely sleep in a bed. Having had so many surgeries in my life and with all the metal screws and wire that hold my legs together, lying on my back or on either side is not just uncomfortable but downright impossible. With limited muscle on the outer aspects of both legs, the screws and wire end up gouging into soft tissue and nerves. So my "king size" bed is a simple "serfs size" recliner.

As I leaned back in my chair and settled in for the night, I began to think of all the things that needed to be done the following morning. We would need to leave early because the drive to Maud, Texas would take about three hours. With Sunday school starting at around 10:00 AM, I would need to have all my equipment set up, and sound check done by 9:40 that morning. We should be on the road by six in the morning, I thought; it didn't look like I was going to get a lot of sleep. That would be nothing new for me.

5:00 AM came early: way too early. There was a time, back when I was touring in country music, that I would have sworn to you five o'clock only came in the afternoon. In all of secular music there is one constant truth; musicians and singers "don't do mornings". But since the Lord had delivered me from that life style, I didn't have that excuse to fall back on when Nena said, "Boyd it's time to get up!"

I lowered my recliner into its upright position and then tried to stand up. The pain that hit me almost caused me to collapse. I fell back into my chair, unsure what had just happened. For me to experience sharp jabs of pain through my hips and legs, had over the last few years become predictable. There were positions I could move my legs into that I knew without a doubt would produce pain, so I knew them well and tried to avoid them; but just standing and putting weight on my right leg was not one of them. This was something new, and it not only felt like it could be a catastrophic event; its timing was also very poor.

My head was spinning as my mind thumbed its way through my list of symptoms. I quickly tried to cross-reference the pain's insignia so that I could reach a diagnosis, and then, ultimately, a quick fix. I knew instantly that it wasn't arthritis because the pain was more prevalent with weight bearing then just movement alone. "Old Arthur" and I had become close friends over the years and I knew that this pain was not a "calling card" from him. It seemed that my knee wanted to bend about three inches higher than it was anatomically possible for it to do so. All I knew for sure was that I would not be putting any weight on this right leg for a while.

I called out to Nena and Brock so that they could help get me into the shower. It was too late to cancel my appearance at Faith Community Baptist Church because they would not be able to find a replacement at such a short notice. I would have to figure out a way to fulfill my commitment to them in spite of what I was going through. As I sent my son up into the attic to retrieve my crutches, I said a prayer that God would give me strength to get through the day.

With considerable help from my wife and son, I was able to get into the car and start the three-hour drive to Maud, Texas. Before leaving our home I placed a call to my parents. I informed them of what I was experiencing and asked if they could meet us at the church in order to help Brock and Nena drag me from the car. It was hard enough getting in to the car and after a three-hour drive I knew what would be waiting for me when I opened the door to get out.

How was I going to get through the day? I didn't know. I just knew somehow that I would. I had been preaching about God's grace being sufficient for so long, that I realized I was now facing yet another opportunity to prove it. Sometimes God leads you into places, or He steers you headlong into situations where, at the end of the day, you are left with only two options; either move forward and prove what you believe, or retreat and eat your words. This was one of those situations and I wasn't anxious to chew on those precious words found in *2 Corinthians 12:9*.

I made it into the church and up onto the platform, but that would be as far as I could go. After the sound check had been done, I didn't have enough strength to get back down off of the stool I was seated on; so I just remained there, waiting for Sunday School to be over and for church to start. Any movement of my right leg would send a searing pain up my femur. It was as if the bone was flexing and moving into areas it was not intended to invade.

Picture in your mind a very small twig pulled from a tree. A twig that was very green inside. Because it's green, you can bend that twig into shapes that a dried twig would not go. But, over time, the outer layers of that twig begin to crack and splinter as the internal layers become exposed. I was beginning to feel as if the femur just above my right knee was being pushed to that same splintering point.

I don't know how I did it. Only by the grace of God was I able to put aside the pain and concentrate on the music and message. It always seemed to me like God just reached out His mighty hand and threw the "pain switch" into the off position while I was singing or talking about His love for us. I believe He was removing all obstacles so that my mind might be receptive to His Holy Spirit and not be distracted by physical things. When the service would conclude, and after my songs had been sung and the message had been delivered, then and only then would the switch be turned back into the "On" position. Then the pain would quickly follow.

This was how it was for me that Sunday morning at Faith Community Baptist Church. I don't know if God moved in the lives of those that were present by what I shared that morning. I do know, however, that through what I endured, God let loose within me an unrestricted pouring out of His sufficient strength and sustaining mercy.

We left immediately after the morning service and drove back home. I would have liked to have gone out to eat lunch with my parents that day, but the "switch" was again turned on and the pain was rearing its ugly head again, so we focused on getting me home to the safety and seclusion of my chair.

That night I tried very hard not to move. I stayed as still as I could in my little "bed-chair" because any movement at all made it feel as if my thigh was being torn into two pieces. When pain can invade the unconscious state brought on through "deep rem sleep", you know you're hurting. Reaching the bottom of your reserved strength and the top of one's pain threshold all at the same time is not a good thing. It's like having a one-track mind with two trains running on it, and you don't want to be anywhere close on the day they come together.

It was early afternoon on Monday. I had managed to get into the car and drive to Brock's Middle School to pick him up. I was in so much pain I found it hard to keep my emotions intact. Brock helped get me back into the house, and then left me in my chair to go and do his homework. I was glad he wasn't there to witness the coming together of those two trains. He didn't see my hands as they began to shake, or hear me as I cried out to God for more strength. Oh, how I begged Him to take the pain away. I even tried to reason with God over all the concerts Southern Grace had coming up. "Lord, you know I can't do them in this condition." I said. But the pain just escalated until my strength was gone and I was crying and moaning uncontrollably. I had surpassed my breaking point.

I don't remember Brock coming into my room but the look I saw on his face, when I opened my eyes, told me he had been listening to my moans and cries for longer then he wanted to. "Daddy, do you want me to call 911" he asked. I shook my head, no, and squeezed his hand to let him know it would be okay. I didn't really believe it would be, and by the look Brock gave me, neither did he. My son abruptly left my room, and I found out later he had gone straight to the phone to call his mother. "Mom," he said, "you have to come home right now." Nena told him she would be getting off work in another forty minutes but that was not good enough for Brock. "Mom, dad is hurting real bad and you have to come home NOW." Nena knew it was bad by the frantic tone in which Brock yelled at her and with an, "I'm on my way," she quickly hung up the phone.

I was in complete and utter agony. I had no concept of time as I faded in and out from under this dark veil of pain. At some point I looked up, and saw Nena and Brock coming in to the bedroom and Nena had a phone in her hand. On the other end of the line was my surgeon and friend, Dr. Vergil Medlock. He told her that, "if Boyd is hurting to the point where he can't handle it, then it has to be bad, so get him in here to Baylor Hospital as soon as you can." Vergil said he would call the E.R. department and tell them we were coming, and that he would meet us there. It was Monday evening, and with the sun going down it had begun to rain. With Nena driving, we headed out for the Baylor Hospital's emergency room in downtown, Dallas, Texas.

The man I had once assisted and stood shoulder to shoulder with through countless surgeries had indeed called ahead. After we arrived, I was quickly ushered into a room where batteries of tests were already ordered. X-Rays, bone scans with radioisotopes and blood work; they would all occupy my first night at Baylor Hospital. But it was the pain medication that Vergil had ordered that ultimately created peace in my mind and body. I had no doubt that Dr. Vergil Medlock would get to the bottom of what had happened to my right leg, and I also knew that if, in the end, he couldn't fix it, he would find someone who could.

Twenty-four hours after being admitted we had the answer to why I could no longer walk. I had been hobbling around since Sunday morning with a broken femur. It had broken just three inches above my knee. Normally this would be an easy fix. A simple surgery with four to six screws and a fracture plate would do it. Yes, if I were only normal, but with me nothing concerning my legs had ever been normal. This would prove to be no different.

I had a metal rod from a previous surgery in Phoenix, Arizona, which ran through the middle of my femur and almost all the way down to my knee. It was the femoral component to my fifth total hip replacement, put in by Dr. Hedley. Over the last eighteen years, the rod had begun to move inside the bone, and each time it did it chipped away pieces of the cortical bone, the part of the bone that provides strength for the femur. This process would eventually cause the end of the rod to push its way completely through the side of the bone. On Sunday morning, June 27th, each time I had tried to put weight on the leg or even move my leg at all, the rod would push through the fracture, further splitting the bone higher and higher up my femur.

"This is something I can't fix," said Vergil. I knew the magnitude of what we were looking at here. The extra complications of existing screws and femoral rods would create great difficulties for any orthopedic surgeon. They would have to undo what was already done by previous surgeons, and then find a way, if it could be done, to reattach all of the hardware of the pre-existing work after they finished with the new work. It would be like trying to build a new skyscraper around the existence of one that is already crumbling down. To find a solution for this would take someone who was proficient in "out of the box" thinking and creativity. Fortunately for me, Vergil had found just the right person to take on this case.

Dr. Nathan Gilbert was a new surgeon to Orthopedic Associates of Dallas and his specialty was tailor made for this situation. He was an Orthopedic Oncologist, a surgeon who specialized in the treatment and reconstruction of bone after bone cancer. It was common work for him to take on the difficult and uncommon cases. Vergil was convinced that this surgeon could find a way, where there was no way. I took a deep breath, a little saddened that Vergil had stepped back and essentially withdrawn himself from the case, but I knew if Vergil was convinced that Dr. Gilbert was the man for the job, then he was the man.

I had grown to trust Vergil with my life and I had already placed my life in his hands one time before in the reconstruction of my left hip, barely five years earlier. I was now placing my life in unknown hands. But in the back of my mind I kept hearing God's small voice whispering to me, "Don't worry, I've got this."

It is amazing how God puts people together, in the right spot at the right time, in order to accomplish the things that only He could foresee. There is no such thing as luck. It's not luck that places you in the right place at the right time. It is He who held the stars in the palm of his hand that moves the pieces of our lives into place. Dr. Gilbert was not there when I worked as a P.A. for Dr. Medlock. He had not yet started his practice when I had my left hip reconstruction by Dr. Medlock and Dr. Lancaster. No, Dr. Gilbert appeared in my life just when I needed him the most. He was there, right where God intended for him to be, at this time in his life and mine. Yes, God did indeed have me covered.

Dr. Nathan Gilbert was a young man, confident in his surgical abilities. You didn't have to talk to him for very long to become aware of that. He also was very down to earth and very much like Dr. Medlock in his delivery and demeanor. I was so pleased to learn all of this on that Wednesday afternoon when he and his P.A., Ms. Samone Chism, came to my room for a formal meet-n-greet.

How surreal it was that Dr. Gilbert's P.A. would be working with him on Dr. Vergil Medlock's past P.A. and that she would currently have my last name. Man, when God is in control and moving all the pieces into play; you just can't make this stuff up.

Dr. Gilbert laid out his plan on how he wanted to approach the reconstruction of my right leg. His theory, and one that he had only tried twice before, was to fix the fracture by using a combination of one long piece of cadaver bone graft coupled with an extra-long fracture plate. His surgical approach to this would be to take a tibia bone from a cadaver and split it in half-length wise. He would make an incision from just below my hip socket to all the way down past my knee. The incision would need to be that long to allow the long tibia graft, now in two pieces, to be placed into my body in its entirety. The split tibia would then be "sandwiched" over my brittle and thinning femur. "If there is not enough bone left inside the femur to keep the metal rod from fracturing it, then we will reinforce it and thicken the femur from the outside," he told me.

Dr. Gilbert would then attach the grafts to my femur through numerous surgical screws and wire struts. The final step would be to attach a custom made fracture plate that would run from mid-thigh to the outer aspects of my knee joint. The plate would be held in place with screws and wire running through the tibia graft and anchored by seven long surgical screws that were to be drilled through my knee.

In theory this would aid in the dispersal of weight and pressure from the already weak and thinning femur and transfer it down, across and into my knee joint. If this worked it would help prevent any future factures due to stress, which would most certainly come to the surface over the next few years. Of course, he had never before tried this with someone who had all the metal, screws and wire from six previous total hip replacements. Although he could overcome that variable in his head, doing it physically, well, that would be something else altogether and would have to be figured out once they got in there.

Thinking on your feet and outside the box was Dr. Gilbert's calling card. There was one thing, however, that he was concerned about. One thing that, if done wrong, could destroy not only his work but all the work from the previous surgeons as well. Dr. Gilbert looked at me and simply said, "We have one major goal here, avoiding Pandora's Box!"

I understood exactly what the "Pandora's box" comment was referring to. If they had to go into the socket area of my right hip for any reason whatsoever, what they expected they would find waiting there could lead to the total failure of this surgery, and quite possibly result in the total amputation of my right leg.

If they had to remove the hip socket component to my last total hip, they knew there would not be enough of my own bone left to repair it. Dr. Gilbert would then be facing the same problem Dr. Medlock and Dr. Lancaster faced with my left hip just five years earlier.

During the total hip replacement that I went through eighteen years earlier, they found huge holes in the socket where bone had broken off and dissolved. They were able to patch the holes using a paste made from ground down bone and surgical cement. The "patch work" was then held in place with several long pelvic screws. If all of this had to be removed, the hole would then be so large it could not be fixed. What was lurking inside "Pandora's Box" was simply a big old sloppy kiss of death; and with this surgery scheduled for the next day, none of us figured we would be in a "kissing" mood.

I was not only disappointed over where I now found myself, but I was also disheartened over where I didn't. Don Peace was busy canceling and rebooking concerts that Southern Grace was supposed to be at. Understanding that an emergency is just that, "an emergency", and something that is never planned for does not lessen the disappointment from those churches and venues that had gone to great lengths to advertise for their upcoming event. Would we be able to reschedule? How much damage to Southern Grace's reputation had all of this caused? I didn't know, but I did know I couldn't think about it now. Hopefully, God would grant us the opportunity to make it up to those who were let down. I'd have a better idea if any of that would be even possible, once the next twenty-four hours had come and gone.

My mom and dad came to make sure Brock was taken care of and that he could get back and forth to school. Knowing he was in great hands allowed me to not worry as much about how all of this was going to impact his life. Between my past surgeries and his own major surgery, his life had been on a large enough rollercoaster as it was without me adding an unexpected turn. But through it all, Brock recognized who it was he needed to lean on. I knew if he found himself craving more of that "blessed assurance", that he would most assuredly receive it.

I was taken to surgery at ten o'clock in the morning on July 1. The surgery would last approximately three hours. Most surgeries into the hip are done by using a lateral approach. This makes it possible to separate each muscle and then retract it to get to the next muscle and so on and so on until the bone is exposed. Doing it this way allows for less muscle damage and shortens the recovery time. This however would not be how my surgery would go! Because the donated tibia (a.k.a. shin bone) would need to be inserted into my leg in two complete full-length pieces, then the incision would have to go straight through all of the muscles. My right leg would have to be opened up wider than ever before. All that muscle damage would mean only one thing; my recovery would be a long and difficult one.

Thank God for the morphine pump! It was my friend for the seven days I spent in the hospital after surgery. My right leg was swollen to twice the size of my left. My right knee was in utter shock. I'm sure it wondered why it had been so abused. It had always been a normal knee, not like the hip that stood right above him. I'm sure it had to have felt violated as those seven three inch screws were drilled through the middle of it.

I had lots of visitors and phone calls in those seven days after surgery. So many people and church congregations were praying for my recovery and I was blessed to be witnessing the outpouring of their love for me and my family. Big Al LeConey (Southern Grace's bus driver, product manager, part-time bodyguard and full time friend) made his way to Dallas to come check on his "little buddy". Only Big Al (who from this point on will be affectionately referred to as "Skipper") could ever get away with referring to me as the "Little Gilligan" of Southern Grace! He and Roy Dale, along with the rest of the group, had diligently watched over me during the last year and a half. I knew in my heart that after all of this, their protection of me would be even greater; well, it would if I could ever get out of this hospital and then back onto "The Blue Goose" that is.

Roy Dale Bray also made the trip to Big D to spend the day with me. It was the second or third day after surgery. I could always depend on him to bring a smile to my face and return laughter to my heart. We sat and talked about absolutely nothing, but to me, just having him there was everything.

Before Roy Dale stepped into my room for our visit, I had just returned from radiology, undergoing a test to rule out a blood clot. Dr. Gilbert and the staff at Baylor were concerned about the swelling in my right leg and wanted to make sure it was not being caused by a clot. Just prior to leaving my room, I was told to 'push' my morphine pump, as the pump would need to be disconnected for the trip. My nurse would then reconnect it immediately after I returned to my room. I knew how uncomfortable those radiology tables were, not to mention how cold, so I happily pushed the pump to give myself a buffer to withstand the trip.

When I returned, I punched my call button to let my nurse know I was back in my room and that I needed the pump to be reconnected. It was then that Roy Dale stepped through the door and into my room.

An hour into our visit and I was beginning to hurt, and the pump had not yet been reconnected. I called the front desk again, and was assured someone would be there shortly.

The second hour came, and I was trying hard not to let my pain show to Roy Dale, so I put in another call to the front desk. "We will inform your nurse. Thank you for calling" was basically what I received in response. I asked, "Well if it's going to be any longer, could I just get some oral medication to help in the interim?" I'll check with your nurse, was the reply. I thought to myself, "Oh you mean the same nurse who has been M.I.A. for the past two hours? Good luck with that!"

As bad as I was feeling, I felt even worse for Roy Dale. He was trying to make me feel better by his visit and now he had to watch me go through all of this. Roy Dale could only sit at the end of my bed and feel helpless.

I had been waiting for three hours. I needed a nurse, any nurse but I would have settled for someone from housekeeping if they would only reconnect the morphine pump, or give me a shot; or even hit me in the head with the mop bucket! "Please won't someone just put me out," I thought.

When the phone rang in my room, it was Nena on the other end of the line. She was checking in and didn't have long to talk because she was calling from work. I told her how long I had been waiting to see a nurse, and she said she'd call the front desk and promised that she'd get somebody in there.

Nena called the main hospital line and asked to be transferred to the nurses' desk on the orthopedic floor. When the desk clerk answered, Nena asked to speak with the nurse that was taking care of her husband. The clerk had to retrieve my nurse from all those urgent nursing duties that were obviously occupying her time in the nurses' break room, so that Nena could talk to her. Nena tried to be nice, as she asked why her husband had not seen his nurse in over three hours. Why had his morphine pump not been reconnected when it should have? Why had his request for pain medication fallen on deaf ears?

The nurse (who will remain as nameless here as she was vacant there), quickly interrupted Nena and in an "I don't believe you tone" said, "This is the first I've heard of it." Nena said, "He has been calling the front desk every thirty minutes for the past three hours, aren't you getting your messages from the desk clerk?" Before Nena could inquire further the nurse (who now has no name) began to be quite ugly and bristled as she said, "Ms. Chisum, I can either go give your husband some pain medication or I can continue to talk to you; which one do you want me to do? You choose!"

If Nena could have reached through the phone and grabbed nurse-no-name by the throat she would have. Nena's direct and professional demeanor went out the window in an instant and turned to a fiery redhead's righteous indignation. "Put your supervisor on the phone right now," Nena demanded.

In just a short amount of time, the nursing supervisor came on the line. Nena quickly ran through the previous conversation and recounted how ugly She-Who-Must-Not-Be-Named had been to her on the phone. Before the conversation went too far, Nena said, "Let's just wait and we'll talk face to face. Tell nurse no name I'm on my way down there… and hell is coming with me." Oh wait, that was Wyatt Earp that said that. What Nena actually said was, "I want a new nurse assigned to my husband's room and under no circumstances was what's-her-name to be allowed back in his room."

If the truth were told, "nurse anonymous" had probably forgotten where my room was anyway. In my opinion, for the sake of the patients and their health at Baylor Hospital, that nurse needed to be shown the "front door"; and I know one long legged redhead who was ready to escort her there.

The rest of my hospital stay was relatively uneventful. It was surprising how fast my call light was answered from that day on. Sometimes they were there before I even punched the button! When we finally left the hospital, I think Nena could have run for the position of CEO of Baylor. And, after she showed the depth of her management and negotiation skills; I have no doubt she would have would have gotten it.

Two months later found me back at Baylor Hospital. My knee was not moving due to all the trauma and scar tissue. I was still not able to walk on it. I could not extend it completely or bend it past thirty degrees. If this surgery was ever going to be a success, they were going to have to tear out the scar tissue in order to get it moving again. After less than an hour under anesthesia, Dr. Gilbert had torn away, twisted off and pulled loose, any and all adhesions and scar tissue in my right knee and thigh. I went home that same day realizing that, in just a few more months of rehab, I might just have a leg to stand on.

CHAPTER 12

From A Broken Vessel To A Masterpiece

I have heard it said that the dash that separates the date of your birth and date of your death will say it all to those whom you leave behind. Make no mistake, we will all make a mark in this world and when we leave, we will leave a legacy behind; the question is, will the legacy you leave behind be viewed as a good one or a bad one?

The Apostle Paul referred to our life here on earth in terms of it being a race, so that dash between the dates on your tombstone now takes on a spiritual meaning as well. There is a race here on earth. What did you do with your dash? What did you stand for and who did you live for? In the end, all the answers regarding the quality of the life you lived will be found in "the dash".

Why is it that so many Christians are like me? In my younger years I was too busy to serve God. I lived for what I could get out of life and not for what I could give to "The Giver of Life". Now, like so many others, wisdom has come with grey hair and sore creaking joints and I don't have the strength to do now what I should have been doing then. Please Lord; forgive me for all the wasted time in the early years of my "dash".

I have, however, spent the past twenty plus years listening and responding to "the call." Just like the apostles did two thousand years ago, I dropped my earthly nets on the seashore and became a fisher of men. I stopped singing in bars, clubs and concert halls. I stopped chasing the sins of the flesh, wallowing in the pride of life and turned from my wicked ways and started my life all over again.

I have run across people who knew me back in the days that I recklessly stumbled in darkness, and everyone one of them has said to me, "You're not the same guy you were back then." I tell them that it's *"by the grace of God I am what I am." (1 Cor. 15:10 NKJV)* Trying to change the complexion and direction of your dash is never easy to do, but I am proof that all things are possible for those who love the Lord and are called according to His purpose.

In looking back on my life I have done things both good and bad and I have also touched lives in ways that will be remembered both well and poorly alike. I have become concerned in the last few years about leaving a positive legacy. In giving something back, leaving something behind that will change and touch lives for the glory of God long after I am gone.

Over the past ten years I've written books, recorded award nominated songs and sung for the glory of Christ, all across this country. All of those things may play a small part in the legacy I leave, but the biggest part of me that I will ever leave behind as a gift to this world, will be found in the six foot two inch frame of my son Brock. The way in which he lives his life going forward, will cast a searchlight that always looks back, and reveals just how he was raised and the degree to which he was loved. He is the greatest part of the legacy I will leave. If I fail him in how he is prepared for this world, then any other successes I have had will mean nothing. What and who he becomes will in the end be mine and Nena's opus and no other accomplishment will mean as much or last as long.

Whether we know it or not, we are our earthly parent's legacy. This realization fills my heart with both sorrow and joy. I am sorry for the years I failed to represent the quality of my raising, but joyful that both my parents have lived long enough to see me standing on the right road, for the right reason and at the right time.

There are times when legacies collide. When one person's life story merges with another's and then together they collectively touch lives in ways that could not have been imagined; when that happens it becomes a God Thing. Only He could cause those diverse paths to cross.

In this final chapter, I will tell the story of such a collision. This is a true story of how God can take that which the world might be tempted to throw away, and then with a master artist's touch, He reshapes and repaints and transforms it into a masterpiece. A new picture emerges from the old by the Masters Hand, and it's signed in His blood and framed in His glory. In the halls of eternity there hangs a beautiful picture of a broken vessel now mended and saved by Grace.

~

Jimmy Roberts was born August 29, 1946 in a little community called Hobson, nestled just a stone's throw away from Chatom, Alabama. Jimmy looked healthy to all of those who were there for his birth. He was the third son of Devation and Molly Roberts and weighing in at ten pounds he was certainly their "large" bundle of joy.

Six weeks after his birth, Jimmy's mom was in the process of changing his diaper when she was startled by the sound of little Jimmy's leg breaking in half. The screams that followed were screams that would return to her ears for years to come. From six weeks old to sixteen years of age, Jimmy Roberts would suffer more than two hundred broken bones. He had a rare condition called Osteogenesis Imperfecta. This condition is a bone disease causing bones to be very brittle and easily subjected to fracture. His bones were so sensitive; so thin that even crawling on the floor as a baby left him with multiple broken bones.

As if his burden in life was not heavy enough, when Jimmy was 3 years old his mom, Molly, was diagnosed with Leukemia. She lived two and a half years longer than any doctor at the time thought she would, and it was her tremendous faith in God and the love she had for her family that sustained her to the very end.

The last toy his mother ever bought Jimmy was a little plastic, toy piano with 10 keys. Oh, how proud he was of that piano. From that little piano, Jimmy developed a love for music. He learned to play *"When the Roll Is Called Up Yonder."* It was a song he would play for his mom over and over in her last days. For Molly it was a proclamation anthem of things to come. She did not realize it at the time, but in those last days she was planting a seed for a Ministry.

Jimmy, along with his two older brothers (who did not suffer from Jimmy's bone disease) went to live with their grandparents after Molly's death. Eventually Jimmy's dad remarried and started another family. Jimmy and his brothers stayed on Grandmother and Granddaddy's farm until their dad and step-mom moved to Florida and then Jimmy's two brothers moved to Florida with them. Jimmy stayed with his Grandparents.

Jimmy's Grandmother quickly picked up where his mom left off. She was determined that he would develop the talents and gifts that God had given to him. In spite of every doctor saying that Jimmy would never live to see his twelfth birthday, his Grandmother would stiffen her spine and set her jaw and tell them, "God gave me this baby and I know he is going to live."

Jimmy wasn't able to go to school like the other children because the school had stairs and steps, and back then there were no ramps and virtually no help for the handicapped. His grandparents taught him as much as they could as they drew from their own limited education. Jimmy's grandmother taught him to use his hands. Everything she thought he could do with his hands she taught him how to do it. She and Jimmy's Great Aunt Esther even taught him the art of quilt making. Jimmy sewed quilts and then sold them for $3.00 each, thus enabling him to save enough money to one day buy his first "Real Piano". His mother's ministry seed was still growing.

One day Jimmy's grandmother got a job in the lunchroom at the local school. She was then able to take Jimmy to public school for the fourth, fifth and half of the sixth grade. Half way through the sixth grade school year, the school bus Jimmy was now riding on had a wreck one evening and this violent crash left Jimmy with numerous fractures. From that day on Jimmy was not able to attend public school.

Jimmy had a thirst for knowledge and he began to read everything he could get his hands on. He went as far as studying schoolbooks all on his own with no real teacher.

When Jimmy turned sixteen he was referred to the Vocational Rehabilitation Service and was sent to live at the Rehab Center in Mobile, Alabama. This turned out to be the turning point of his life. Because of his education, or lack of a formal record of one, Jimmy was given numerous tests to see how much education he really had. When it was all over, Jimmy amazed everyone. His test scores showed him to have the equivalent of a two-year college education.

At the young age of sixteen, Jimmy was sent off to Business College where he took classes in accounting and general office work, including office machines and typing.

While attending Business College, Jimmy was able to come home from time to time, mostly on weekends. On one weekend trip home, the local church was in revival. Jimmy decided to attend their Sunday morning service. He would end up giving his heart to God just two weeks later. With the filling of the precious Holy Ghost, Jimmy never ever again suffered another single fracture!

Jimmy would forever be in a wheelchair and that was understood by all. He would never walk or run a single step on this side of time. God would show the world, however, through Jimmy, that you don't have to stand on your feet to be a Minister of the Gospel, Singer of Grace, husband to a wife, father to a family, or a grateful child to a Heavenly Father. All you need is a willing heart to follow where God leads and God will take care of the rest.

After Jimmy finished Business College, he returned home and went to work in the office of the local factory in Chatom, where he labored for 40 years as an Office Manager.

When Jimmy was around nineteen years old he started playing the piano for the Journeymen Quartet. This was a dream come true for a little boy who first started playing piano on a little plastic toy. He worked Monday through Friday and then traveled with his music ministry every weekend. His mother Molly, now in heaven, had to have been so proud of who and what he became, as well as "Who" it was he now served.

On January 21, 1972 Jimmy met the love of his life at a singing in Fairview, Alabama. There was no doubt in his mind that God had made Debbie just for him. They courted for a while and then married on June 29, 1972. She ended up being everything a wife could possibly be. God truly knew what He was doing when He gave man a helpmate, because Debbie became a vital part of Jimmy's ministry.

A little over three years after they were married, God gave them a beautiful little girl they named Aimee Cherie. Sadly, Aimee was born with a broken leg. So little was known about Jimmy's bone disease at that time, and they had no idea it could be passed down to their children. No one in Jimmy's family had ever suffered from that condition as far as anyone knew.

God gave Aimee to Jimmy and Debbie, and they believed she served her purpose for being born. Aimee also suffered from a heart defect that the doctors had not found, and so she went to be with the Lord on September 13, 1975. She was their little precious baby and Jimmy and Debbie both knew they would one day see her again in Heaven and on that day she wouldn't be wearing a cast.

October 21, 1976 God gave Jimmy and Debbie a son, Timothy Wayne. Tim did not suffer from the bone disease that his sister and father suffered from. He was a fine healthy boy weighing in at nine pounds and six ounces.

On April 2, 1979 Brian Scott was born. At the time of his birth they were told that he did not have the bone disease. But, at three weeks old, while Debbie was giving little Scott a bath, she heard that familiar pop and then the horrific scream that followed. Sadly for Scott it was a scream that would be heard time and time again over his lifetime.

Each time that Scott suffered a fracture it was as if Jimmy was being broken all over again as well. Jimmy knew the pain that Scott was feeling and that only enhanced the closeness between him and his son.

Imagine having the fear that just by holding your child you could end up terribly hurting him. Jimmy was now experiencing the same fear his mother Molly had, but he also had to keep in mind the fear of his own propensity for fracturing. Jimmy put aside his fears and never failed to be there for his son; and Debbie, bless her heart, she was there for all of them. In spite of the pain, the many hospital visits, surgery after surgery for little Scott, God gave this family a joy that very few families ever experience.

Jimmy's grandmother had been told that he would most certainly die before he reached twelve years of age. As it turned out, all those clairvoyant doctors are dead now! Jimmy outlived them all and is still on the road for Jesus.

There are doctors, and then there is *THE GREAT PHYSICIAN!* Regardless of your diagnosis, never get the two confused.

Scott Roberts was a hyperactive child. Jimmy and Debbie could have raised him in a "padded bubble", but not only would that have not been much of a life for Scott; but he'd probably have found a way to get into something that would cause a break even in there. Scott thought that every child took a trip a few times a month in the middle of the night to the Mobile Alabama Hospital. To him this was a normal life and surely everyone had the pleasure of experiencing what he was going through. It wasn't until he grew older that he realized how "differently-special" he really was.

There were countless trips made both in the light of day and the darkest of nights, down Government Blvd. to the hospital in order to get Scott the help he needed for the fractures he was suffering. Arriving at the hospital was always the worst part of the ordeal. No one ever handled Scott with the gentleness or tenderness of his mother. That's not to imply that the nurses or security guards that always met them in the Emergency Room parking lot were intentionally rough, but there is no touch like a mothers' touch.

It was on one of those occasions, when after the ER staff had pulled Scott's broken body from the back seat of the family car and placed him on a gurney, that Scott began to scream out in even more pain than before. A powerful voice rang out from somewhere behind them demanding, "Someone put a pillow under his knee so that it's not flat on the bed." That voice came from a heartbroken father, rolling behind Scott's gurney in his own small wheelchair. As soon as someone placed a pillow under Scott's knee, the pain became bearable again, and Scott thought to himself, "My dad is the smartest man in the world." Of course, all his insights and brilliance came with a very high personal price.

When Scott was six years old he was lying in a hospital bed in his parent's living room. It had snowed in South Alabama, which was extremely rare if it ever happened at all. Just as the snow fell down and blanketed the ground, the excitement fell down as well upon all the children in the neighborhood, including Scott. Then he realized, as beautiful as it was and regardless how loud it had called out to him to come and play, that he couldn't. Scott watched from his bed, heartbroken with the realization that the hard white full body cast he was now in would be as close as he would get to that soft white fluffy snow outside.

In the corner of the living room was a little 10 key piano. Scott looked at his fingers and thought to himself, "They've never been broken." His mom brought it over and placed it on top of Scott's Spica body cast. Just as his father's journey into music had begun many years earlier, so would Scotts'. God used music to comfort Scott and to be his closest friend. He banged and pecked on that piano every waking hour. Scott played along with the records and cassettes of all his favorite Southern Gospel groups. Of course his favorite was his dad's group, The Journeymen.

Scott's favorite musician was the piano player from the Kingsmen, "Anthony Burger". He tried to match Anthony's' every "lick", failing miserably most of the time, but having a wonderful time nonetheless.

Soon Scott would take his melodica (a little wind instrument with keys on it) to the singings where the group his dad was playing for at the time was performing. They would let Scott play during the offering time. Occasionally Scott would even sing a song or two like, *"He's Still Working on Me,"* or *"Mansion Over the Hilltop."*

When Scott was in the fifth grade the doctors told Jimmy and Debbie that their son should never attempt to walk because his bones were just not strong enough to hold him up. Because of Jimmy's talent in sewing, he made all of his own clothes and he made Scott's as well. This talent came in handy, especially when Scott needed custom made clothes to cover large and heavy casts. Jimmy would fix all of Scott's pants with Velcro so that Scott's Mom could easily get him dressed. God certainly "handpicked" the right man with the right talents and experiences to be Scott's father.

Scott was between the ages of ten and eleven when his dad started their own family Gospel group called The Ambassadors. Scott was expected to sing tenor for the group but he didn't have any idea of how to do it other than to sing a higher note than anyone else did. But when he opened his mouth to sing at that first family rehearsal, it was as if he had been singing tenor his whole life. God's like that you know! He often shows his miracles disguised as coincidences and accidents. The world should not be fooled by either. God is always in control!

It is amazing how we as human beings can talk about things that we have no firsthand knowledge of. Oh, we were told by so and so, or I believe it's true because my parents said it is, but we really don't know if it's true because we've never experienced it ourselves. There is head knowledge, which is that that we've learned from others, and then there is heart knowledge, truth that has touched you personally! Scott was about to learn the difference.

Did you know that God doesn't have any grandchildren? That was a question that Scott heard in church one Sunday morning when he was twelve years old. The message that morning rang clear as a bell to Scott that "just because mom and dad went to church and are saved doesn't mean you get grandfathered into heaven". It's a personal thing, a relationship thing, A *FATHER CHILD THING*!" So when the Pastor essentially asked the congregation that morning, "Who's Your DADDY", Scott rolled his wheelchair down to the front to be introduced to Him *"personally"*.

In 2004, Scott was asked to join The MaHarreys Gospel Group as their keyboard player. He toured with them for five years playing piano, singing harmonies and lead. His time with the MaHarrys helped take the group to two top eighty national record releases. That, which had its humble beginnings back on that snowy day lying in a hospital bed in his parents' living room, had turned from heartbreaking to chart breaking as his gifts were now being heard on a national scale.

It was during those five years of touring that Scott began to feel more disabled than he ever had in his whole life. Up until then, Scott had only felt "differently-abled." Now he found it increasingly difficult to negotiate his wheelchair on and off the tour bus. Maneuvering his chair around all the cords on the MaHarreys concert stage was difficult as well. Being confined to a chair was becoming increasingly problematic.

At a Sunday morning church service in Arkansas, a Pastor approached Scott and told him that he had been praying for him and that he just knew God was going to strengthen his legs. He said, "I believe God will, but it's going to require you to step out on faith before He does." After the church service, Scott shared the prophetic word he had received from the Pastor. The MaHarrey's had been invited over to have lunch with one of the church families that day. As Scott shared the story with the group and the family around the lunch table, he heard one of those family members say, "Hey, we have a rolling walker out in the garage!"

Scott wanted to test "the word" that the Pastor had been given on his behalf, but fear is always the devil's playground. Scott had not attempted to walk since he was in the second grade, an attempt that didn't end well at all. Could this really be happening? Did this pastor really hear a word from God? There was only one way to find out.

Everyone gathered in the garage to see what would happen. They were all anxiously watching and breathlessly praying as Scott attempted to step out on faith, both spiritually and physically. The first full trip around the garage was tense-filled, but the second was all smiles and rejoice-full!

It was late that night when Scott made it back home to his parent's house. Jimmy and Debbie were already in bed asleep. Scott brought the walker that the church family had given him earlier that day, into the house and left it in the living room for his dad to find in the morning. Scott's father woke him up early that next morning asking, "Whose walker is that in the living room?" Scott boldly replied, "It's mine!" Scott then proudly took hold of his walker and walked around the house for all to see. Jimmy Roberts cried. Through his tears he said, "I never thought I'd ever see the day that you could walk."

The events of that morning in the Roberts' house cause me to remember another crippled man. He sat outside the gate called "Beautiful" begging for silver and gold. The Apostles Peter and John walked by on their way into the temple to worship, as the story goes, in Acts Chapter 3, when this crippled man caught their attention. Peter told the man at the gate, who was crippled from birth, *"Silver and gold I don't have but what I do have I give to you: In the name of Jesus of Nazareth rise up and walk."* Can you imagine how the crippled man's family felt when they returned to retrieve him from the gate that evening only to find him up, walking and rejoicing in the temple? I am sure that that scene bears a stark resemblance to what was going on in the living room of the Roberts' household that glorious Monday morning.

I know that even today there are times it hurts Scott to walk on his legs, using his walker. But Scott is the kind of "servant" who will never sit down on what God has given to him. He just pushes on through the pain; leaning on the walker he has named "The Scott Rod". For someone who is barely four foot tall, with braces on both legs, I know it's only his love for God and the strength *of God* that keeps him on the road for Christ. In my book, that makes him a "Giant" among men.

Scott met Lisa over lunch in May of 2008. Lisa was the new lead singer for the group "Pardoned" and Scott had been invited to come meet her the next time the group made its way into Alabama. It didn't take long after that first meeting for Scott to start plotting and scheming on how to steal her away. They started dating and over the next year Scott finally figured it out; he asked Lisa to marry him. They were married on the 10th of January 2009.

Scott continued with the MaHarrey's for the next five months, but it was obvious that God had a vision for Scott and Lisa. In June of 2009 Lisa and Scott formed their own group, "Broken Vessels," and together they stepped into a ministry that God is blessing beyond measure. Since June 2009, there have only been seven weekends that Lisa and Scott weren't out there singing for God somewhere.

Southern Grace had been asked to sing at the Deep South Quartet Convention. Penney Talley was putting all this together and she had contacted me to see if we could do the event. Her husband and son are members of "The Crusaders," and this was an evangelistic outreach, co-sponsored by The Crusaders Ministries and the Unity Baptist Church in Hope, Arkansas. A three day event designed to reach the lost, touch those who are hurting and to lift up in prayer those groups participating and to empower them to continue God's call on their lives.

Penney Tally had heard about my song, *I'll Run With You,* and after seeing a YouTube video of it, felt the need to share it with two individuals who were also in the Christian music ministry. They also suffered from physical disabilities themselves, one of them never having walked a step in his life. So the song, speaking about running in heaven, would be especially meaningful to him. The song *"I'll Run With You"* had a powerful touch on Jimmy and Scott Roberts, and I was moved and honored to get to know them through the sharing of that song.

A collision of legacies has happened. All three of our lives have come together; lives that span different decades but still have so much in common. We've suffered physical hardships beyond most peoples' ability to comprehend but, along with the hardships, struggles and pain, we were also given a gift. The gift of music mended our hearts and gave rise to a song in our soul. It was the one thing that helped each one of us to make it when so many thought we wouldn't. I believe that God never allows something to be taken away without giving you something even better to take its place. However, with such a gift comes a responsibility to use that gift to the glory of the "Giver" of that gift.

As the song says, *"I may limp up to the gate but I'll run on the other side."* But I know it won't be just me. We're all going to limp up to the gates because we are all broken vessels. My Bible says all have sinned and fallen short of the glory of God. The brokenness of my body and Jimmy, Scott and Myrtles' as well, is just more visible than most, but there are those who hide their scars. Some are broken spiritually or emotionally and they live their lives behind a "storefront façade" pretending that all is well. But I want to tell you that there's a gift waiting to be claimed. The gift is that of peace in the midst of turmoil, comfort in the throes of pain, and eternal salvation for a lost and all too temporary life.

In early March 2011, Scott Roberts and I will be in the studio, recording a duet version of *"I'll Run with You"*. The anointed message in this song will continue to touch lives long after God has called me home. It will be sung by those who have not only earned the right to sing it but have lived the kind of life to appreciate the miracle message within it. Are *you* ready for the race?

Myrtle Jordan, Jimmy Roberts, Scott Roberts and I will one day join Lacee Johnson and together we'll run those streets of gold forever. Don't miss "the race" you were made to run, the race that ends at the feet of *your* savior Jesus Christ.

Will you be our running partner?

EPILOGUE
"The End of the Beginning"

I slowly open my eyes. With a big gasp, I breathe in air so pure that it actually makes my lungs tingle. And, with that eternal breath I realize the lack of something. For the first time in all of my memory, there is no pain. No constant, dull, droning pain radiating throughout my hips, back and knees. All I feel is the warmth that seems to be radiating through my pores and in every fiber of this new body.

With each step I take, I feel closer to this place I have not seen; a place of final destination that inaudibly calls to me. I have stepped over time to a place where time is no more and where my faith will finally end in seeing.

This cane that I carry in my hand is of no use to me now. I carry it like a child would carry a stick, swinging it back and forth, chasing the wind with it but having no need to put weight on it. I hold it up and see the well-worn handle, now shiny and smooth from years of friction, over all the days and nights that I had struggled to walk. But here on this side of time, all broken things are healed, and empty things are filled. Yes, now it's just a stick with a hook, and that's all it will ever be.

Just over the next hill, I can see the gate. The path that leads to the gate is narrow and straight, but as I follow where it leads, it is obvious that many have come before me because the path is worn from the countless souls of those who have finally come home.

I glance to my left and see what must be thousands upon thousands of wheelchairs strewn about, much like children leave their toys. Wheelchairs of all shapes and sizes left abandoned and in a hurry, as if their owners literally leapt from their seats while the wheels were still turning. I turn to my right and see miles and miles of walkers, standing silent with no one to guide them. There will be no need for shuffling and timid steps here. So with boldness, they were left to stand silent and unneeded, just outside the gates.

My steps quicken as I get close to the walls surrounding heaven. I can reach out and touch those walls of jasper, walls that tower upward into heaven itself. I stand in awe as I see that the foundations of the walls are inlayed with precious stones, sapphire and emeralds, for as far as my eyes can see. One step more and I've reached the Gates of Pearl.

Peering through the gate I see glimpses of what awaits me just on the other side. I see the glow from the streets of pure gold, yet they are so pure they are like looking through glass. I see light that shines from everywhere and has no end, no dimness. There seems to be no night, only the radiant Light from a Risen Lord.

My hand reached out to swing wide those pearly gates, but I could not go in. The cane that I held tightly in my hand could not cross over. That cane was a dying symbol of my old body, and it could not enter here. It had been such a part of me all these many years that I almost couldn't let it go. Now I understood the sea of wheelchairs and walkers and why they were stacked up along the path. I can see why there were mountains of eyeglasses and hearing aids and forests of green oxygen bottles. I understood why they were left behind, because I am a new creation, not only in name and spirit but now in body as well. I can't help but smile as I think of the power that I now see in the Resurrection of Christ as it plays itself out in me.

So, I took one last look at this scarred up old stick, calmly hung it on the gate, and stepped forever inside.

Inside the gates I hear music. Music in languages I did not understand and yet somehow I knew what they were saying. I could hear melodies emanating from all directions almost as if it were being carried along by a gentle breeze.

Then I heard a voice singing soft and low. A voice I had heard many years ago as a young child, a voice that back then was weak with age but now it was strong and pure. It blended in with the sound of old time harmonies as this small, "Appalachian Madrigal" began singing a welcome home song just for me: *Beulah Land.*

I look to see where those heavenly voices were coming from. I saw standing arm in arm, my Grandpa and Grandma Hatfield. At their side stood Uncle Marlin, Aunt Sweetie, Uncle Hump and Aunt Maxine. As they all continued to sing, I could see standing just to their right Uncle Leo, my sweet cousin Cindy, Uncle VA and Wade. Just as I went to hug them I caught a glimpse out of the corner of my eye and there was Papa and Grandma Chisum along with Ricky, Uncle Jerrel, Uncle Frank and Jerrel Wayne. Oh, how they all looked so healthy and happy. It seemed that the entire family of those who had gone on before me, the ones that I had known on earth, had collectively gathered just inside the gate, to welcome me home.

I moved from one hug to another, from one hand shake and smile to the next, until I found myself looking down that golden street as it wound its way down past mansions so grand I could not believe my eyes. As I stood there, breathless from this beauty that lay before me, I heard someone saying, "Holy, Holy, Holy," and then quickly I realized those words of praise were coming from my own lips. It was beyond anything I could have ever hoped for or imagined.

From the road ahead I saw two figures making their way to me. The first was a man I had not seen in my life on earth and yet I felt I knew him. Just behind him walked a beautiful young lady, who was carrying something, but she was still too far away for me to make out what it was that she held so close in her arms. As the man approached I could see him smiling and he slowly began to clap his hands. As he reached out to take my hand, I knew his name; it rolled effortlessly off of my tongue. He said, "Welcome home Boyd," and I replied, "Thank you, Job."

We talked for a moment about how great it was to be home and how the trials of our lives on earth were so small compared to God's riches in glory, that He so freely had given to us. Job looked at me with eyes that already knew the answer to the question he was about pose: "What is it you want to do first, Boyd?" I looked at him with a smile I could not wipe away from my face and declared, "I want to run!"

With that, Job stepped aside and this beautiful and tall young lady that had been waiting behind him stepped forward and in her outstretched left arm she handed me what I had only ever dreamed of; a pair of heavenly running shoes. I looked at them and, as I marveled at their beauty, this young lady spoke to me saying, "Hello Boyd, my name is Lacee Johnson and I've been holding these just for you." I quickly put them on as my heart began to beat faster. "Where do you want to run first?" asked Lacee. Without missing a beat I asked, "Where is Jesus? Let's run to Jesus."

We ran together down streets of gold, through crowds of people shouting "Hallelujah!" and "Praise the name of Jesus!" I ran so fast my lungs were aching and my legs were burning but I did not grow weary. I could feel the wind as it blew through my hair. It brushed against my face like a feather from one of heaven's angels, caressing cheeks that had seen their last tear.

As we ran, I noticed we were picking up more and more running partners for this, my first yet final race: a race for me that would never end. And I could hear them encouraging me to run faster. "You can do it Boyd! Run Boyd, run!"

As this band of runners crested a hill I could see a glow in the distance. It was a glow that surrounded the figure of Jesus Christ, and He was waving for me to come. As I got closer, all the runners I had picked up along the way began to slow down, as if they realized this was an important time for me and one that I needed to experience alone.

As the distance between us narrowed I could hear Jesus calling to me, "Come, let me hold you in my arms, come and I will give you rest!" As I fell breathless at His feet, I could feel his nail pierced hand on my shoulder and I heard his voice say to me, "Stand up. Well done, my good and faithful servant: rise up. I have always been Your Running Partner."

~

As you read this version of how I imagine heaven will be, I need to tell you that the Bible says no man has seen nor ear heard the wonders He has prepared for us in heaven. So, this is just a small sample of "my vision" of what awaits those of us who know Jesus as our personal savior.

But I need to ask you this before you close this chapter of your life. Do you know for sure, where you stand, could you look me in the eye and say for certain that you will be my running partner in heaven? You can know with certainty before you close this book. Bow your head and pray with me ~ *"Lord Jesus, I know that you came to set me free. I know you died on the cross to buy a pardon for me so that I may have everlasting life. I ask you to come in to my life: be my running partner here on this earth and forever in eternity. Please forgive me for my sins, and it's in your Holy Name I pray, Amen."*

OK NOW, "LACE UP YOUR RUNNING SHOES AND I'LL SEE YOU AT THE STARTING LINE…JUST INSIDE THE GATES.

THE

BEGINNING

BUY A SHARE OF THE FUTURE IN YOUR COMMUNITY

These certificates make great holiday, graduation and birthday gifts that can be personalized with the recipient's name. The cost of one S.H.A.R.E. or one square foot is $54.17. The personalized certificate is suitable for framing and will state the number of shares purchased and the amount of each share, as well as the recipient's name. The home that you participate in "building" will last for many years and will continue to grow in value.

Here is a sample SHARE certificate:

YES, I WOULD LIKE TO HELP!

I support the work that Habitat for Humanity does and I want to be part of the excitement! As a donor, I will receive periodic updates on your construction activities but, more importantly, I know my gift will help a family in our community realize the dream of homeownership. **I would like to SHARE in your efforts against substandard housing in my community!** *(Please print below)*

PLEASE SEND ME _____ SHARES at $54.17 EACH = $ $_____

In Honor Of: _____

Occasion: (Circle One)   HOLIDAY   BIRTHDAY   ANNIVERSARY

   OTHER: _____

Address of Recipient: _____

Gift From: _____   *Donor Address:* _____

Donor Email: _____

I AM ENCLOSING A CHECK FOR $ $_____ PAYABLE TO HABITAT FOR HUMANITY **OR** PLEASE CHARGE MY VISA OR MASTERCARD *(CIRCLE ONE)*

Card Number _____ Expiration Date: _____

Name as it appears on Credit Card _____ Charge Amount $ _____

Signature _____

Billing Address _____

Telephone # Day _____ Eve _____

PLEASE NOTE: Your contribution is tax-deductible to the fullest extent allowed by law.
Habitat for Humanity • P.O. Box 1443 • Newport News, VA 23601 • 757-596-5553
www.HelpHabitatforHumanity.org